D0830039

THE EXPERIMENT

Screw

Cupid

the sassy girl's guide to picking up hot guys

Samantha Scholfield

THE EXPERIMENT
NEW YORK

The Experiment, LLC

260 Fifth Avenue

New York, NY 10001–6425

www.theexperimentpublishing.com

Library of Congress Control Number: 2009925218

ISBN 978–1-61519–000–3

Cover design by Michael Fusco | michaelfuscodesign.com

Author photograph by Hugh Hamilton Photography

Design by Pauline Neuwirth, Neuwirth & Associates, Inc.

Manufactured in the United States of America

First printing September 2009

10 9 8 7 6 5 4 3 2 1

To those who think it's lame to wait for
the Hot Guy to come to you—
this is for you.

Contents

Introduction
why you, the sassy girl, need to read this book

Most of the dating population seems to be under the impression that girls have it easy in dating. Supposedly, all I have to do as a chick is flash some killer cleavage and flip my perfectly wavy hair, and the hot men will come a-runnin' with drink offers, dinner invitations, showers of diamonds, and trips to Fiji.

But what happens if your boobs aren't capable of anything close to "killer cleavage," and the persistent cowlick in your hair, however adorable your mother finds it, negates any possibility of perfection?

Such feminine wiles may work if you happen to be one of those lucky bitches who have not only won the genetic lottery but have secured the funding to surgically enhance said winnings. I, unfortunately, am not one of them.

Don't get me wrong—I don't think I fell off the ugly tree. Other than sometimes (OK, oftentimes) wishing my boobs were bigger (A cups unite!!), I'm generally content and happy with my lottery loot. However, when I can't swing a rattlesnake and not smack five of these ridiculously beautiful freaks of nature, it's difficult to get the hot men to notice me and my un-cleavage-a-rific A cups.

Not being the patient sort when it comes to boys and getting asked out on dates, I decided at the early age of thirteen that waiting around for a movie/ice-cream invitation from the Nirvana-obsessed boys I lusted after in high school just wasn't going to work for me.

At first, I sucked. I completely freaked out many of my male peers by bucking the apparent trend and asking them out (also known as picking them up) first. I'm well aware I've left a trail of confused and weirded-out guys in my bungled pickup wake.

However, after many years of failed attempts, mixed in with some pretty awesome success stories, and many, many hours spent testing my theories, I can say with much certainty that I know my way inside, outside, on top of, and all the way around the art of pickup.

This book details the cringe-worthy but hilarious failures on my personal quest to conquer the ego-trouncing mountain of pickup knowledge, as well as the golden moments of glowing success. It then segues into my best attempt at a definitive how-to guide for us girls, detailing exactly how to get from salivating after the Hot Guy you just spied across the room all the way to setting up the first date, no matter the situation or location (including figuring out if he's a "good one" who you potentially may want to keep around for awhile). I've also included a section on what Hot Guys look for in girls (based on interviews with a sampling of real, live Hot Guys), and a section on what you, the hot, sassy chick, need to figure out about yourself and what you want before you have too many dates to know what to do with them all. (Hot Guy, by the way, refers to any guy you personally find ridiculously attractive. This and some other useful terms are defined in the glossary in the back of the book.) Basically, I've tried to make this book the how-to guide I wish I'd had when I figured out waiting for the dudes to make the first move wasn't my dating modus operandi.

Over the years, I've actively tried to make as many mistakes as possible—to get them out of the way and learn as quickly as possible what works and what doesn't. If I've met my goal with this book, by the last page you will have no doubt as to how to pick up any Hot Guy of your choosing in any situation. You will also have laughed out loud with me and at me, thought that I was a genius, thought that I was an idiot (in a "What was she thinking?" sort of way), and most of all, wholeheartedly agreed with me that waiting around for the Hot Guy across the bar to come and talk to you is the lamest thing EVER.

Crap Advice: *Stand with a group of your girlfriends in the corner of the bar and wink at the hottie across the room. If he's worth going out with, he'll come to you.*

Why Is It crap? Any guy delusional enough to approach a large group of girls waiting for attention in the corner of a bar is either completely wasted or a cocky asshole with an overinflated ego.

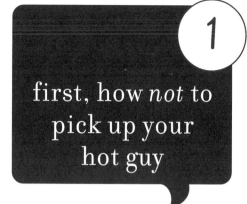

first, how *not* to pick up your hot guy

My First Proposition . . .
FROM THE CAPTAIN OF THE CHESS CLUB

THE first boy I remember hitting on me was named Tommy Drew. He threw sand in my face during recess when we were in kindergarten. Later that night, while helping me attempt to remove the excruciatingly painful and persistently lingering sand particles from under my eyelids, Mom explained that little Tommy accosted me because he liked me. Although I was extremely skeptical, she continued to say that if he didn't like me, he wouldn't have bothered to temporarily blind me in the sandbox; he would have totally ignored me. Although this seemed completely counterintuitive, without any prior experiences that contradicted her statement, I was forced to accept that she had superior knowledge in the matter. I personally would not have chosen that particular method to express my affection, but I was "with it" enough at the tender age of six to realize that boys were a completely different species. So, if Mom said that when little Tommy threw sand in my face it was a token of his affection, I was willing to accept it as truth.

As I got older, it became slightly easier to determine whether or not boys liked me—although their chosen methods of communicating their interest remained a mystery. Take sixth grade, for example: a certain Hot Guy named Matt Lawrence apparently "liked" me, and he let me know by writing a note explaining his intentions and giving it to his best friend, Joey. Joey, as Matt's best friend, messenger, and liaison, passed it to my best friend, Katie (and thereafter messenger and liaison), who then gave it to me. The note read, "Will you be my girlfriend?" I, who had not actually had more than two-word exchanges with Matt up to that point (although I found him to be an excellent example of mid-nineties Hot), and this being my first experience in the girlfriend role, decided to live on the edge and take the plunge. I wrote "Yes" on the note and gave it to Katie, who gave it to Joey, who then gave it back to Matt, who then apparently accepted my response by telling Joey to tell Katie to tell me, "Cool."

Days one and two of our "relationship" continued in a similar fashion; in other words, Katie and Joey relayed such messages as "You look pretty today" (to me, from Matt), and my response to him, "So do you," which resulted in an agonizing ten minutes immediately thereafter while I waited for his response. I wasn't sure if calling a boy "pretty" was acceptable, even if he did indeed look especially "pretty" (in a manly, Hot Guy way) that day. Luckily, at my insistence, Katie was able to glean from Joey that Matt "definitely smiled" upon receiving my response. Whew!

Screw Cupid: The Sassy Girl's Guide to Picking Up Hot Guys

On day three of our relationship, still not having spoken to Matt face-to-face, I received another message, this one in a verbal format. Katie relayed a question from Joey, who had forwarded the question from Matt: Would I like to go a movie with Matt and his dad? I, being grounded at the time for eating the entire crust off Mom's apple pie, was unable to accept his invitation and was forced to relay this sad news back to him through the proper channels. I was then informed via Katie that Matt, upon hearing of my home detention, decided that he didn't want a girlfriend who couldn't go see movies, so he told Joey to tell Katie to tell me that he was not my boyfriend anymore, and that was that. There was no heartbreak involved, at least on my end, as I had not actually spoken to Matt in person during our relationship.

As the years went by, it seemed that most of the boys with whom I came into contact arrived at the conclusion that directness was the preferred method of communication. It became abundantly clear who liked whom, why, what they wanted, and when and where they wanted it done. Take Brandon Stewart, for example: in a particularly poignant moment when we were in tenth grade, he shouted at me, "Hey! You're really hot—why don't you come give me a blow job in the bathroom!" Not having the ninja retort skills I do now, I shouted back at him, "Yeah . . . you wish!"

Or Nathan Gandle, president of the chess club, who approached me very seriously after physics class one Thursday and informed me, "I'd really like to have sex with you. When and where would be a good time for this to happen?" After Brandon Stewart's charming blow job invitation, I rather appreciated his respectful approach, so I added a "Thank you" as a delayed afterthought to my knee-jerk response of "Never."

I began to wonder—was this what my love life was going to be like? Was every one of my future dates going to involve requests for sexual favors in the bathroom? What if I didn't like any of the guys who got up enough guts to deliver their lines? And by extending that, what if the guys I did like—for example, a certain Hot Guy named Ryan Masters, who had transferred to my school and into the seat directly in front of me in Civics—never asked me out?

Ryan Masters:
MY FIRST (VERY PUBLIC AND VERY HARSH) REJECTION

It seemed, based on my experiences thus far, that if I didn't want my high school years to be doomed to propositions of sexual favors, I had a decision to make. I could either wait around for Ryan Masters to come to his senses and approach me, or I could take matters into my own hands.

I wasn't too keen on the waiting-around option. So far, my contact with Ryan had been brief and not overly discouraging, but there wasn't much encouragement, either. The first time I talked to him, he politely acquiesced to my request for a pen, but then he disappointingly went back to his business of drawing boobs on his notes. The second time I spoke to him, I asked for a piece of gum, having moronically forgotten to lose my pen before class. He responded in the negative to my request, not having any gum on him at the time, and again went about his business with no further interest in me or my gum shortage, while I was left silently cursing my idiocy at not asking for something I was sure he had, like paper. I wasn't entirely sure if he was aware I existed.

The more discouraged I became as a result of Ryan's non-interest, the more it seemed as if taking the initiative was the only solution. If I wanted action, I was going have to take the bull by the horns.

However, it appeared there were some obstacles.

The first and biggest obstacle was that I appeared to be the only girl in the history of the universe who had ever even considered broaching the apparently forbidden barrier of initiating conversation with a member of the opposite sex. I had thoroughly surveyed my female friends, their female friends, and their female friends' friends, and I had arrived at the unfortunate (for me) conclusion that not one of them had ever asked a guy out; none had ever even thought about asking a guy out, and none had ever heard of any other girl asking a guy out—except in movies. It appeared that a) the age-old tradition of man talks to woman and not vice versa reigned supreme in my tiny universe, and therefore b) I was clearly charting uncharted territory and was going to have to reinvent the wheel on my own. This led me to my second obstacle.

How on earth was I going to do this? I could certainly extrapolate from my personal experiences and predict that yelling "Hey Ryan! How about coming and making out with me in my car?" would not garner me much respect. And using the direct, assuming approach like Nathan Gandle, chess club aficionado, made my knees quiver in fear. There was no way either of those approaches was an option. But what else did I have to draw from? I racked my brain but remained clueless about how to approach the godlike Ryan without risking either unthinkable rejection and/or intense humiliation.

I tried saying "Hi" one particularly brave Wednesday during Civics class, in the hopes that this was all it would take for him to profess his love. But all he did was look at me with an expression that clearly said, "Why are you talking to me?" There was no "Hi" back.

Since my initial attempts hadn't yielded me the Friday-night flowers/dinner/movie/confession-of-undying-love combination I was hoping for, I moved my efforts up a notch.

In a plan I considered to be fiendishly clever, I let a few choice members of our school's gossip mill know that I "liked" Ryan. Our prom queen/captain of the cheerleaders had always announced to the lead gossipers who she wished would take her to the school dances, and without fail the gentlemen in question would follow suit and ask her to the specified occasion after only a few hours. If it worked for her, it would work for me, right?

Unfortunately, and to my utmost embarrassment, all the gossip mill did for me was ensure that every time I walked through the main quad during break, I was guaranteed to hear at least two variations of "Sam and Ry-an sit-ting in a tree, K-I-S-S-I-N-G. . . ." To be completely honest, although the taunting was embarrassing, I didn't particularly mind the mental image the song conjured up. In fact, I rather liked it. Ryan, however, started making it a habit to avoid me at all costs, even going as far as to sprint into the boys' bathroom whenever I entered his general vicinity. I guess he correctly assumed this was the only place he could go where I couldn't follow him—at least not while maintaining any modicum of respect for myself.

I found myself at a loss. Civics became an hour of incredibly depressing hell as I was taunted by the sight of his back and shoulder muscles moving under the fabric of his tight, striped polo shirt whenever he took notes and doodled boobs on said notes.

I moped through my daily activities, not really paying attention to the things that used to make me happy. Without confirmation of Ryan's affection, what was the point of life?

So when I finally discovered the answer to my all-consuming problem, I was beyond ecstatic.

My epiphany occurred while I was in the student government office, absentmindedly taking care of one portion of my duties as student body treasurer by perusing the covers of those school promotional magazines in which they try to pass off thirty-five-year-old women as school-spirit-crammed high school juniors. I stopped on one particular cover—which looked like it had been photographed in 1985—when I saw it:

SADIE HAWKINS DANCES—
TURN THE TABLES TO INCREASE ATTENDANCE.

Here was my answer! I wouldn't have to forge new ground because *everyone* knew that Sadie Hawkins dances were where the girls asked the guys, not vice versa. All I had to do was convince my fellow student leaders that a Sadie Hawkins dance absolutely needed to happen, which I did the very next day during our meeting.

Shockingly, my idea was received with extremely little enthusiasm. For some reason, none of the other girls seemed to like the idea of being forced to ask a guy out. I pitched my case with more enthusiasm than I had ever given anything treasurer-related before. I couldn't give up the true reasons behind my enthusiasm without sounding like a total dork, but I tried every trick I had to convince them that this was such an amazing idea—it would be the end of our high school microcosm if it didn't happen.

Finally, by threatening that we would not have enough money for the new and highly lusted-after candy bar vending machine without the dance, the motion passed. I had won.

I planned with gusto what was going to be my perfect night, making sure that the entire student body knew what the deal was with the invitation protocol. In this way I hoped to set the scene in no uncertain terms, so that there would not be one iota of possibility that Ryan could think it was weird when I asked him to the dance.

I personally felt that I was being very subtle, but I guess it was pretty obvious to the general student body what my ploy was. It had leaked from the student government meeting that I had been the one to push the dance through the voting. It didn't take a genius-level IQ to put together 1) the public knowledge that I liked Ryan and 2) the fact I had conceived of the dance, and conclude that I had created the dance for the sole purpose of asking Ryan. So much for subtlety.

The taunting in the quad increased exponentially as we got closer to the date of the dance. Ryan stopped coming to the quad altogether and, disappointingly, disappeared from the campus scene. I coped with this new development by reasoning that he had seemed shy during Civics and therefore perhaps couldn't handle the extra attention. Whatever the explanation, I didn't care. I was riding on a cloud. I'd put so much time and effort into my plan, no other outcome besides success was conceivable.

Exactly one week before the dance, I decided to put my plan into action: on this momentous Friday, I would ask Ryan to be my date. I saw the whole interaction perfectly in my mind—he would act surprised that a girl such as I was interested in him, respond to my perfectly delivered and flawless invitation with a hugely enthusiastic "Yes!" and then tell me that he had secretly been harboring intense feelings for me from the first day he had arrived in Civics, and would I be his girlfriend? He would then gently place his hands on either side of my face and kiss me in front of everyone.

My beautiful fantasy couldn't have been further from what actually happened.

I informed my then best friend, Julie, that I had chosen today as the Day. Julie, being a sucker for gossip, apparently found it impossible to keep this information to herself for longer than two minutes, and as soon as I walked away she immediately told Sasha, queen of the gossip mill, that I was going to be asking Ryan to the dance that day. Sasha, who for some reason had never let go of the fact that I had beaten her in a harmless game of dodgeball in first grade and had hated me ever since, jumped on this tidbit with all the violent hunger of a shark finding that a particularly plump seal had strayed from the group. As far as I could gather from the rehashing of events the following week, the lovely Sasha told as many people as possible, as quickly as possible. This was big news in our fishbowl of a school, since I'd been in the spotlight ever since my crush had been put in the public eye. The feeding frenzy had reached a fever pitch by the time morning break rolled around and my time to ask Ryan the long-awaited and much-anticipated question arrived.

The break bell rang, and I accompanied the butterflies having violent seizures in my stomach on a walk across the quad. I didn't see Ryan, which wasn't that big a surprise, considering his recent penchant for hermitlike behavior. Everyone was watching me walk around, looking for someone. Again, given the information at hand that 1) I was asking Ryan to the dance that day, and 2) he wasn't to be found, the unanimous conclusion was that I must be looking for Ryan to ask him to the dance. I guess that's why every tenth person I passed informed me with a wink, "Hey, Sam—Ryan's in the gym," or some variation thereof.

Once armed with the information I needed—namely, his whereabouts—I walked purposefully away from the quad and toward the gym. An extremely excited pack of forty or so of my gossip-addicted peers followed me not so subtly to the stairs that led to the gym and its adjoining field. My audience waited at the top of the steps as I boldly continued down to the gym entrance, searching for Ryan. When I finally saw him, he was walking rather quickly across the field outside the gym in a direction that took him as far away from our spectators as possible.

His high rate of speed and direction of retreat should have set off alarm bells, but unfortunately for me, I was still firmly ensconced in the mind-set that nothing could go wrong. I didn't think anything of bellowing "RYAN!" as loud as I could to stop him so I could execute my plan. As my screech reached his ears, I thought I saw him flinch but wasn't sure if I had imagined it. What he definitely did was stop and turn toward me, which I took as encouragement. As I jogged the excruciating sixty feet to where he was standing, I noticed that he rather resembled a trapped animal who has conceded his fate. Again, I failed to translate this.

"Hey, Ryan. Wow . . . it was really hard to find you!"

(Looking at the ground) "Yeah . . . I know. I did that on purpose."

"Um . . . oh. Well, anyway, I wanted to find you to ask you

. . . if you, uh . . . um . . . ifyouwantedtogotothedance-withmenextFriday?"

"You wanted to find me to ask me what? You're mumbling. . . ."

Shit. I have to say it again?!?! "Oh . . . um . . . sorry. Um, well . . . I wanted to find you to . . . ah . . . ask you to be my date for the dance next Friday."

(Then he looked at me. The butterflies had almost reached the back of my throat and were threatening to escape in a flapping torrent the next time I opened my mouth.)

"No."

What?! He must be joking. I had come too far and put too much effort in for this not to work.

"No? . . . Ah . . . well . . . it's going to be great. I planned it and everything."

"Yeah, I know you planned it. That's why I don't want to go."

(Still not fully comprehending what was going on, I forged forward, with forced and, I noted in the back of mind, somewhat high-pitched laughter emitting from my throat.) "Why, because my decorating skills aren't up to par?"

"Uh . . . no. Because I don't like you like that. And I really wish you'd stop stalking me. It's weird."

Ouch. It was only then that I really caught his drift. Actually, saying that I "caught" his drift isn't accurate. His drift slammed into me like a tractor being dropped from an airplane, sans parachute. I didn't have anything to say. I just stood there and stared at him in disbelief.

He walked away, leaving me in the middle of the field. To the salivating fans standing above us on the stairs, I'm sure it was abundantly clear what had just taken place. Complete silence confirmed this theory when I stumbled back up the stairs to the quad to get my books. No one said a word.

And that was my first rejection. It was brutal.

Looking back, perhaps my method of letting approximately eight hundred people know that I liked Ryan had backfired. Perhaps claiming him as my date to the dance prior to asking him wasn't the best situation I could have put myself in. Perhaps being so consumed with my goal that I ignored all obvious red flags wasn't the most intelligent way to approach a solution. That said, I still felt his "stalker" name-calling was totally unwarranted. My impression was that stalking someone involved at the very minimum driving by their house as frequently as possible. And I hadn't done that. I didn't even know where he lived.

I went to my dance . . . by myself (and actually had an OK time, given the circumstances). The one plus side was that my pet project raised enough money to buy the vending machine, slightly tempering my humiliation with the prospect of a Snickers on hand whenever I felt so inclined.

Hot Barista Guy Hank:
MY FIRST SUCCESSFUL PICKUP

It took me awhile to get up the nerve to approach another Hot Guy after being burned by the no-longer-godlike Ryan Masters. By awhile, I mean about eleven months, which in high school was an eternity.

The Hot Guy who caused me to come out of mourning my stomped ego was this amazing-looking guy working the coffee bar at my local Starbucks. To gain accessibility, I conveniently developed a certain obsession with vanilla-nonfat-no-whip-with-two-Equal lattes and found an excuse to go to Starbucks almost every day. Once there, I would bask in the Hot Guy glory that was the coffee guy, soaking up every second of the ten minutes I could squeeze out of my latte run. Any more than ten minutes and I figured people would have a very valid reason to accuse me of stalking.

After about a month of this, I finally gathered enough courage to talk to Hot Barista Guy longer than my standard "Hey, how's it going—I'll have the usual. . . ." My knees were shaking as I waited in line, trying very hard not to look like my knees were shaking. I was sure that everyone there knew what I was up to. He and another girl were taking people's orders, and I had to do some quick maneuvering with the guy behind me to ensure that Hot Barista Guy was the one who took my order. Finally, it was my turn.

"Hey! I'll get my usual. . . ."

"Sure thing . . . that's five seventy-four. TALLDOUBLENON-FATNOWHIPTWOEQUALLATTEFORSAM anything else?"

"Uh . . . I've never gotten your name. What is it?"

(At this point I notice, like the genius I am, that he's wearing a name tag.)

"Oh! My name's Hank." (He smiles and points to his name tag.)

(Here comes my big moment . . . by far the scariest moment of my life up to that point, especially now that I understood so well exactly how bad rejection could be.) "OK, Hank . . . um . . . I was wondering . . . um . . . whatyou'redoingon-Fridaynight?"

(At this point, my knees were quivering to such an extent that I had to press them against the counter to keep them from knocking. After a pause probably lasting only half a second—but which felt like about a thousand years—he answered me.)

"What did you say? I couldn't understand you. Did you want a bagel or something to go with your coffee?"

Oh, sweet Jesus, when will I learn to stop mumbling?! "I was wondering what you were doing on Friday night?"

(There! Delivered flawlessly. Now to concentrate on not throwing up.)

"Hanging out with you . . ."

Oh. My. God. Suck it, Ryan Masters! See! Other people like me!

" . . . Let me just go ask my manager if I'm working on Friday."

(He left for twenty seconds and returned to the counter.)

" . . . Yup. Hanging out with you. What are we doing?"

Whoo-hoooooooooo!

"Movie?"

"Awesome. I'm on break in ten minutes—can you hang out here until then?"

Could I ever. I am a GOD! "Definitely."

And I hung out for ten minutes, with a smile that didn't go away for five hours.

My second attempt at taking the bull by the horns had gone better than I could ever have imagined. I, the Ryan Masters reject, was going on a date with Hot Barista Guy Hank, because I had asked him and he had given me the greatest four words of my life: "Hanging out with you." Up to that point, the greatest moments in my life had been 1) the Christmas morning when my parents had blindfolded me and placed in front of me the most beautiful dollhouse I'd ever seen; 2) the previous month, when I had successfully beaten my best friend Andy at wrestling; and 3) when I was eight and figured out one night that I could get away with not eating my peas by strategically squishing them into my mashed potatoes, rendering them invisible to my unsuspecting parents. The magical four words from Hot Barista Guy Hank completely reset the bar and made these previous moments feel like ten-day-old mold. I had never been so elated and so proud. I was awesome, I was amazing, and I was fantastic. No one in the world could have told me otherwise at that point—especially not the guy who viciously maimed Sadie Hawkins dances for me.

I rode my power trip for six days. On day seven, I found out Hank had an ex-girlfriend who was none too happy that she had been dumped for some (and I quote) "latte-ordering bitch." I was forced to take steps toward getting a restraining order because of the month-long deluge of instant-messaged death threats and attempted murder by her trying to run me over in her mother's minivan in the mall parking lot—and I determined that Hank wasn't worth the psycho ex-girlfriend baggage. She was welcome to him.

But even if my relationship with Hot Barista Guy Hank was short-lived, my ego got such a boost, it needed its own zip code. After its previous complete and utter deflation, it was a welcome change.

The Hazards of the Push-Up Bra

When my ego and I went away to college two months later, I felt confident that I had totally figured out how to pick up guys. I figured I had one rejection under my belt. But, much more important, I also had one rock-star acceptance. I felt ready for anything.

I couldn't have been more wrong.

Because I had never been in a bar up to this point, there existed a hole in my information bank where knowledge of picking up guys in this new world should go, a world where some of these guys redefined the word player. They were a sect of males that hadn't existed at my high school. They were smooth beyond their years, they seemingly knew all the right moves, and they were complete and total asses. And they got laid—all the time.

I desperately wanted to fill this void but could not figure out a way to talk to the guys I wanted to talk to while my friends and I were being constantly bombarded with comments like, "So, baby—do you suck on everything like you suck on that straw?"

After I observed a few hundred more smooth moves, my thought progression went something like this:

I'm awesome. Proof: Hot Barista Guy Hank said "Hanging out with you."

I'm good at picking up guys in non-bar atmospheres. (Yes, a bit of an extrapolation after one success . . . in a coffee shop) Proof: Hot Barista Guy Hank said "Hanging out with you."

The players are good at picking up girls in bars. Proof: Laura went home with that cheeseball Mike Saturday night after he told her, "It's OK if you buy me a drink—and nice ass!"

If I model the players' pickup techniques in bars, I should be fine.

Backed up by my very questionable logic, I decided to test out my theory. The next time my friends and I were out bar-hopping, I picked out a guy who easily would have earned a unanimous rating of 9.5 from a female audience. He was sitting at the bar with two of his guy friends, his back to me. I wasn't too nervous—I mean, how badly could I mess up? Hot Barista Guy Hank had said "Hanging out with you."

I walked over to the 9.5 and leaned on the bar next to him, casually (or so I thought) letting my padded bra brush his back in what I hoped was a sexy move. However, I must have misjudged how much padding I had attached to my chest, because when I slid in next to him, I ended up pushing him off his chair. It wasn't such a push that he fell, but it did manage to make him lose his balance and deposit half his drink on the floor.

This was unfortunate for me because there wasn't anyone on my other side who could have been blamed. In fact, there were two empty stools, at the time/space equivalent to the Grand Canyon. The 9.5 whirled around, noticed the enormous gap of air to my right, and to my mortification, instead of the "Hey, Baby" I'd expected (fake boob mishap aside), he said, "What the fuck. God." And turned back to his friends.

You would think that my experience with Ryan Masters would have cured me of any and all tendencies to forge ahead in the face of obvious and complete rejection. Unfortunately, this was not the case. Although I found the 9.5's reaction a bit extreme, my assessment of the current situation was filtered through my current "I can do no wrong—Hot Barista Guy Hank said 'Hanging out with you.'"

I decided in my delusional mind-set that this was the opportune time to use the infamous line coined by cheeseball Mike, the player: "It's OK if you buy me a drink—and nice ass." The way I saw it, we were both clearly skilled in the art of picking up the opposite sex, so if it had worked for him, it should work for me. In retrospect, this was a grossly extreme exaggeration of my skills, but I have to give myself credit for being brave, even if it was at the expense of logic . . . and my ego.

I repeated the magical phrase to the 9.5 and got no response. He didn't even turn around.

Figuring he hadn't heard me, I said it louder: "IT'S OK IF YOU GET ME A DRINK—AND NICE ASS." Once again, I had overshot the mark and ended up bellowing at him instead of merely getting his attention. I also caught the attention of everyone within ten feet of us, who all stopped talking to look at me. The 9.5, who had shrugged his shoulders against his ears during my bellow, turned around and said—excuse me, shouted—"I HEARD YOU THE FIRST TIME."

As he turned back to his laughing friends, I observed that his face had contorted into a look that fell squarely into the camps of both extreme annoyance and utter disgust. It finally sank in after he shouted at me that 1) amazingly, the line hadn't worked. In fact, it had provoked the opposite reaction from what I'd expected. And 2) I'd probably never be able to show my face in the bar again. I think I must have been in a state of shock, because I don't know how I managed to exit the premises without further humiliation, but I accomplished it.

I still blush to this day whenever I think of that moment. It rated an easy 15 on a scale of 1 to 10 and was the single most mortifying experience of my young-adult life, including my rejection by Ryan Masters.

My experience with the 9.5 helped me to arrive at two conclusions: 1) perhaps I needed to take my ego down a few notches, and 2) I really needed to think through what worked and what didn't work.

The answer to the first was easy. The 9.5 had taken care of any and all needed ego-trouncing. If my ego had required its own zip code before, it now needed stitches to stop the life-threatening arterial bleeding.

The response to the second conclusion was a little more complicated. Since I was basing everything I knew about pickup in bar-land on one experience, I arrived at the uncomfortable conclusion that it would behoove me to gather more data. A lot more data. I needed to unearth a way of breaking the ice with the opposite sex that did not involve utter humiliation.

This, of course, meant I would have to go back out onto the battlefield. Unfortunately, at that moment this sounded less enticing than rolling around in a bed full of agitated scorpions. Furthermore, if my one experience was anything to go by, it seemed safe to assume the journey I was planning to undertake was going to have a very steep learning curve. I decided it seemed too masochistic if I made each encounter personal, whereas if I could convince myself I didn't care if I had another experience like the one I had with 9.5, I just might learn something.

What Happens When "Can I Buy You a Drink?" Is Directed at a Hot Guy

The first pickup method I decided to copy belonged to a guy named Damon, who had stood at the bar next to me and asked if he could buy me a drink. Being the opportunistic sort, I wasn't going to turn down a free drink from a relatively cute guy, so I said yes. The drink buying was followed by about ten minutes of fun conversation.

"Can I buy you a drink" certainly isn't the most original way to start talking to someone, but I figured if it had worked with me to at least start a conversation, it was fair game for testing out in the opposite direction. Plus, it seemed very feasible and a lot less intense than telling someone they had a nice ass, which made the approach that much more attractive.

After Damon left, I observed a Hot Guy standing to my left who looked like as good a candidate as any, so I fearlessly delivered my line. Unfortunately, in my cavalier selection process, I had not bothered to notice whether he already had a drink. I immediately became aware of the presence of his current drink when he held it up about five inches away from my nose. Finding this a rude gesture that fed into an already slightly embarrassing moment, I decided he may not have been such a good choice after all and proceeded to look elsewhere.

I located another Hot Guy standing by himself at the bar a few minutes later. His response to my offer: "Why?" There wasn't a "Yeah, sure" or a "No, thanks" that preceded this question. It was just a point-blank interrogation. This struck me as an extremely odd reaction. Wasn't it obvious? Why would he ask to buy a girl a drink? I desperately wanted to tell him, "It goes both ways, genius. I think you're cute and I want to go on a date with you . . . Duh." However, this seemed like kind of a bitchy reaction. Maybe I had just caught him off guard. Maybe he was having a bad night. I couldn't think of an appropriate answer to his question, so I just walked away.

Being an optimist, I decided to try my line again. My first attempt had been botched by logistics and could therefore be removed from the tally. The one bad verbal reaction had to be an anomaly. Who responds like that to someone offering to buy him a drink?

I found yet another Hot Guy at the other end of the bar. He was standing with a group of people but didn't look that engaged in the conversation, so I figured he was pretty accessible. After checking thoroughly to determine that there was no drink present, I made my move.

"That's a weird question coming from a girl—what do you want?"

First off, how do I even answer that question? I don't ask you what you want when you ask to buy me a drink. The answer is obvious—you want to get in my pants. Why would it be any different coming from a girl? And, second, "That's a weird question"? How is that a weird question? Can . . . I . . . Buy . . . You . . . A . . . Drink? I see nothing weird about it. Guys say it to me all the time.

I was completely mystified at this point. Had I stumbled into some secret society of guys who were so completely insular that they couldn't recognize the very tactics *they* used every night in every bar? I decided I would try it on a couple more guys. Maybe what had happened was that I had run into the only jerks in the bar and everyone else would be awesome. If I gave up now, I would always wonder.

Hot Guy number four was about twenty feet away from Hot Guy number three. He appeared to be by himself, very much upping his approachability in my eyes. One Hot Guy seemed infinitely less frightening than two Hot Guys standing together.

I made eye contact with Hot Guy number four before I advanced and was rewarded with a smile. Encouraged, I decided to approach him. He had been observing my bushwhacking attempts to get through the impenetrable crowd that separated us, so when I finally reached him, I got a "Hi—what's up?" with another smile. When I asked him if I could buy him a drink, the smile promptly disappeared and was replaced with an expression of such dismay and horror that I took a stumbling step backward. He immediately leaned toward me and hissed, "What's *wrong* with you?!"

I guess you could say I snapped at this point, because I responded . . . OK, shouted:

"What's *wrong* with me?? WHAT'S *WRONG* WITH ME!!! NOTHING!!! HAS SOCIETY REALLY TRAINED US ALL SOOOOOO WELL THAT IT'S *WRONG* FOR A CONFIDENT CHICK TO ASK TO BUY A GUY A DRINK BECAUSE SHE THINKS HE'S HOT??!! I'VE GOT TWO WORDS FOR YOU, JACKASS—DOUBLE STANDARD!!"

I certainly felt better after taking out my wrath on Mr. What's Wrong with You, but I think he was probably scarred for life, judging by his mimicry of a kicked puppy as he backed away from me and toward his friends during my tirade. Once I was done and was focusing my best death glare on him, he slipped past his friends and into the masses in the bar, leaving me basking in my outburst afterglow. The girl standing next to me gave me a high five as I left, mildly improving the overall success rating of the evening. At least I had peripheral support in my quest.

· · ·

Man Interview:

IT WOULD BE SWEET TO HAVE A GIRL HIT ON ME

The next day, when I consulted my closest and highly trusted guy friends, I was informed by unanimous opinion that: 1) yes, it is weird for a girl to offer to buy a guy a drink, because 2) there's got to be something wrong with her if she's that desperate, and 3) no, the guys I hit on will never believe that I'm not desperate if I'm being that obvious about being interested, so 4) I should basically give up this whole "take the reins" thing.

Great. This meant that the guys I trusted implicitly were also unenlightened.

You would think at this point that my enthusiasm for my self-inflicted quest would be waning, but it wasn't. If anything, my night of rejection had gotten me even more interested. I now knew, if I extrapolated, that guys thought it was weird for a girl to make the first move. Although technically this was a negative fact, I was happy to have gathered valuable information. I also had a stubborn hunch that there had to be some way for a girl to pick up a guy without his thinking it was weird.

I decided to interview some more guys to see if I could crack the puzzle. The more information I had, the better the chances were I'd figure out a solution. Plus, I wanted other guy opinions on the subject, outside of my crazy friends.

I spoke to as many guys as I could, in bars, in coffee shops, in the library, and at the gym, always asking the same question: "Would you think it was weird if a girl hit on you?" After my guy friends' assessment of the situation, I was pleasantly surprised to find that only one guy out of all the guys I interviewed said that he wouldn't like it if a girl hit on him. He told me it "wasn't a woman's place to be doing that." Ugh. The rest of the guys had varying positive responses. A few of my favorite responses are listed here:

"That would be so sweet if a chick digged on me. I'd totally bang her."

(Awesome.)

"The ladies of the world can have the reins if they want them—I would LOVE to not have to pick up girls anymore. Do you have any idea how hard it is? You're all so mean!"

(Oh, if only he knew what I'd gone through!!)

"Why—do you want to hit on me? Because if you do, that'd be fine by me. You're pretty hot. I guess I'd bang you."

(Um . . . thanks?)

So it appeared, miraculously and at least in theory, that I had found a subset of the male population that indeed approved of the girl making the first move. This seemed a total contradiction to my previous in-field experience but was great news all the same. If I knew for sure that there were guys out there who liked the idea of girls hitting on them, I felt confident I could find them.

Using a Dog to Catch a Hottie

Energy and enthusiasm renewed, but still unsure of how to go forward, I turned to Google and the ubiquitous girl-advice magazines. There was a remarkable amount of information about keeping a guy around, finding and experiencing the perfect orgasm, finagling marriage proposals, what to do and not to do on a first date, and a whole plethora of websites instructing guys on how to get laid—but very little information for women on how to actually meet guys. In fact, I only found one article on the subject, which listed of how to meet guys. Unfortunately, nine of these were clearly not meant to be used in reality, or so I hoped for the sake of my fellow readers. If they were serious, I hope no one tried them. The results would be disastrous.

Take example number four: *Send the cutie in the office next to yours a box of chocolates, signed "Your secret admirer . . . who's watching you right now."*

Based on Ryan Masters's labeling me a stalker when I wasn't really stalking him, I shudder to think what the recipient of the chocolates would assume based on that signature.

Or example number nine: *When you walk by the cute guy you've had your eye on, let your chest casually brush his back. He'll be so smitten, you'll have a drink and a date in under a minute!*

Uh-huh. Just be sure he's not sitting on a bar stool, that he's not holding a drink, that you don't push too hard, that your chest isn't too big or too padded, and that there are other people in the immediate vicinity to blame if you get a little carried away with your "casual brush."

My personal favorite was example number ten: *Turn the tables* on him and ask to buy him a drink before he can offer to buy you one. He'll be blown over with admiration for your confident and sexy show of control.

Yeah—and if you pick up an agitated rattlesnake, swing it violently around your head by the tail, and then plant a big wet kiss on its snaky little snout, it won't sink its fangs into your lip, leaving you with several thousand dollars of cosmetic surgery and a lot of explaining.

The one usable example I gathered from this article of fun was: Next time you go running, bring your dog. Then, when you pass the dog-toting hottie you've been admiring, let your dog check out his dog. While they're doing that, you can check out when he's available for your first date.

It wasn't perfect. I didn't actually have a dog, I didn't actually have a "hottie" in mind, and they didn't explain how one got from "Hey, how's it going?" to "Let's meet at eight at that Italian restaurant on Main"—but I figured it was worth a shot. It was better than stalking my "cutie" of a coworker with chocolates, so I decided to try it.

The first order of business was to find a dog to borrow. Only one of my friends had a dog: my flamingly gay and adorable friend Timothy. Timothy had a teacup Chihuahua named Shakespeare. Shakespeare was not the optimal dog for a run on the beach because his legs were only four inches long, but he would have to do. After promising Timothy that I would run slowly and not let Shakespeare impregnate any other dogs, I left for the beach.

When Shakespeare and I arrived at our intended location, I was pleased. From my car, I observed no fewer than four dogs accompanied by guys who could safely be classified as "hotties." Encouraged, I began to move along the sidewalk at the fastest rate Shakes's legs would allow—which was a slow walk for me. I didn't want to tucker him out to the point where he would be too tired to do his dog duty and check out other dogs. After all, he was an integral part of my plan.

About twenty minutes in, I noticed a Hot Guy approaching us. He was also walking, which I thought a better situation than if he had been running, and was holding a leash that was clearly attached to some animal. I didn't bother to follow the leash down to see what kind of dog he had, as the key to my plan was that he had a dog, nothing more. Plus, I was distracted by the sight of his six-pack through his T-shirt as the wind blew against him.

Shakespeare had been merrily strutting ahead of me during our walk, his leash slack. However, when Hot Guy and I got about fifteen feet apart, suddenly Shakespeare's leash went taut. I looked down to figure out why and was pleased to see Shakespeare sprinting toward the Hot Guy's dog. *Ah*, I thought. *My little plan is working!* However, my pleasure was short-lived.

There were two key elements to my scheme that I had failed to consider: The first was the well-known fact that the smaller the dog, the bigger the ego and therefore the bigger the internal misconception about one's actual size. Translated into my situation, Shakespeare thought he was roughly the size of a buffalo. The second element I had failed to verify was that the selected Hot Guy should be holding on to a member of the canine persuasion, and not a member of, say, the monkey persuasion.

Shakespeare reached Hot Guy's "dog," which turned out not to be a dog at all, but a scampering black-and-white monkey. Shakespeare, who, I am sure, had not yet been exposed to such an exotic creature, had stopped three inches away from the monkey's nose and was growling like the mad buffalo he thought he was. I wasn't sure of the temperament of monkeys in general, not having spent a significant amount of time with one, but I felt fairly confident that the cocked head and hissing noise from deep in its throat was not a good sign. Adding to my concern, the monkey looked as if it weighed an easy fifteen pounds, dwarfing Shakespeare by a factor of five.

I decided that it was definitely time for me to intervene. As I covered the six feet between me and the imminent interspecies altercation, hand outstretched to retrieve little Shakes before something bad happened, Hot Guy said to me in a decidedly non–Hot Guy voice, "Please remove your excuse of a dog. It is clearly upsetting Michael." I continued leaning down, at the same time trying to come up with something suitably scathing as a retort, when all of a sudden the monkey reached out its little claws and attach themselves to each of Shakespeare's ears. Before I had time to even draw in the breath to say "Hey!" the monkey pulled with all its monkey-arm strength, eliciting a high-pitched squeal from poor little Shakes.

Through all of this, the no-longer Hot Guy was standing over me, yelling at me not to hurt his "precious baby Michael." His "precious baby," having lost interest in Shakespeare, was now calmly cleaning itself about five feet to my left. Huffing, I got up, still holding on to poor Shakespeare, and loudly asked the guy what the hell he was thinking by bringing a monkey to the beach. He didn't respond, distracted by his tut-tutting over Michael the beast. I checked Shakespeare to make sure he was all right, which besides the shaking he appeared to be, and walked back to my car.

I took little Shakes to the vet on the way home just in case. Timothy would never forgive me for putting his baby in such danger, but maybe he would appreciate the gesture. Shakes turned out to be just fine, but I was not.

I felt I had pretty safely determined that there were far too many factors that could go wrong in that particular plan for meeting my "hottie." Even if I could make it work, was I going to rely on borrowing dogs to meet my future dates? Unlikely. I had to figure out a solution where Murphy's Law didn't have quite as much jurisdiction. The lower the number of factors that could go awry, the better.

As I thought more about my last attempt, it occurred to me that what I liked about it and what made it seem like it might work, vicious exotic animals aside, was the fact that the actual pickup wasn't happening in a bar: it was happening outside. Guys always seemed more accessible to me away from bars. This led my thoughts to other outdoor venues where Hot Guys hang out. Basketball? Baseball? Soccer? All of those involved Hot Guys, but there was the interruption factor to consider. I needed a place where Hot Guys congregated but didn't do very much, therefore making them more accessible for chatting. And that's when it hit me:

Golf courses.

Guys Like Golf. I Like Guys. Golf Is a Great Way to Meet Guys . . . Right?

Almost every Hot Guy I knew played at least some golf. Some were more regular features on the golf course than others, but the vast majority had gone to the driving range at least once in the last six months. How could I go wrong? I could go down to the driving range, ask for some pointers from a cute guy, and *boom*—I'd be having a conversation! From that point, it would be child's play to get a phone number.

I had gone to the driving range a couple of times in the past with my dad but had never really picked up anything that could be called skill. My total ineptitude could only work in my favor, because I really would need some pointers. After all, I couldn't very well ask for pointers if I already knew what I was doing. I borrowed one my golfer friends' drivers and took off for the nearest golf links, bursting with fresh enthusiasm.

I arrived, bought my bucket of balls, and selected an open tee next to a Hot Guy. I caught his eye, smiled at him, and was very pleased to see that he smiled back. I could feel him watching me, and I really wanted to do badly so that I could ask him for help.

I put my ball on the tee and did my best to do a crappy swing. Unfortunately, I hit a near-straight 175-yard drive.

Damn it! I needed Damsel in Distress, not Competent Athlete. I looked to see if the Hot Golfer Guy was still watching—he was not. His attention was focused solely on his ball. I kept one eye on him, hoping he would direct his attention at me again. Unfortunately, this did not appear to be a likely action—he was concentrating so hard on his ball and his face was contorting.

I knew from listening to my dad ramble on about his unruly golf game that the harder you tried to hit the ball well, the more likely it was you were going to mess up. That logic in mind, I teed another ball and concentrated on hitting the ball very, very well, hoping for a very, very bad result. Even though Hot Golfer Guy was totally entranced with his skills, if I hit the ball badly enough, I thought I might still have a chance to talk to him. I could always play off my first drive as a fluke.

As I started to swing my club down, it immediately appeared that my dad was correct in his golfing theory. I was in for an atrocious swing, although not the intended after-effect. Instead of connecting my club with the ball, I totally missed. In field hockey we called this whiffing. I'm not sure what the proper term is in golf, but the end result was that instead of hitting the ball, my club continued in its arc and deposited its full momentum directly into my tailbone.

I don't know if you've ever fallen on (or been hit on) your tailbone, but it basically feels like someone ripped out your spinal cord and poured acid into the open wound. Hitting yourself with a golf club in that same spot is a very similar experience.

Hot Golfer Guy had heard the thump of my club connecting with my backside and was doing his best not to laugh. I found this rather unsympathetic, even though admittedly I had looked like a total idiot.

Since I could hardly walk, let alone continue to swing a club, I decided that perhaps this whole golf idea wasn't the greatest. Hot Golfer Guy had resumed his driving but was still occasionally letting out a chuckle. It didn't appear that my unintentional self-sacrifice was going to help me out with talking to him, so I hobbled out of the driving range and back to my car.

• • •

Am I Dreaming the Impossible Dream?

On the drive home, between grimaces every time I moved any body part that involved my spinal cord, I found myself becoming a bit discouraged.

The dog-walking scenario had been fairly complicated: there was the availability of Hot Guys walking dogs. There was the acquisition of a dog for myself. There was the running versus walking because said dog's legs were too short. There was the setup of making sure the dogs sniffed each other. There was the weather. There was the alternative animal factor. In short, it seemed to me that that particular idea had been set up to fail. Too many things could go wrong.

The golf scenario had seemed less complicated, and yet I had still managed to invoke that asshole Murphy and his stupid law.

Perhaps these situations were just too specific? So many factors had to be in place before any meeting of any Hot Guys could happen. And even if I could fine-tune the dog-walking and the golf so that I could avoid the potential disasters, I couldn't realistically rely on them as my sole dating method. It was all so much work. There had to be something easier that was more reliable.

A few days went by with no brilliant ideas or breakthroughs on my part, and nothing worth using from any of the guys who decided to grace me with their one-liners. I felt myself becoming concerned that maybe there wasn't a way to do this. I hadn't ever seen any other girls, except in movies, who could pick out the guy she wanted to talk to and successfully make the first move. Even taking into account the movies I had seen, on the rare occasions where the woman was doing the advancing, it was because she was an undercover cop or a hooker or something—not exactly applicable to my current situation. Basically, I had never seen happen what I envisioned possible: a fast, reliable, reasonably ego-safe way to talk to the guys I wanted to talk to. My enthusiasm was starting to bottom out. Was I dreaming an impossible dream?

The Epiphany About the Secret of Pickup

That Thursday, as I rode the bus to the local Barnes & Noble to buy a ridiculously overpriced but cool book for my English class, "Sex in Romantic Literature," the relatively attractive twentysomething guy behind me tapped me on the shoulder and asked for the time. I gave it to him and turned back around. I then felt another tap. When I turned to him again, he said he had seen my reading list by accident and what did I know about that class, since he was scheduled to take it next quarter? I replied with what information I had about the class, and a lively discussion ensued about how useless majoring in English is outside of providing fodder for cocktail parties. We decided to continue the conversation over coffee the next day and exchanged numbers. I got off the bus a few minutes later. still chuckling to myself from our conversation.

That's when I realized it: I had a real, honest-to-god date with a cute guy who hadn't started the conversation by hitting on me. He hadn't even planned to talk to me. All he had wanted was some information: the time and the lowdown on my English class, which had led to a fun conversation and exchange of numbers. If this had worked for him, it seemed not too far-fetched an idea that it would work for me as well.

I thought about our encounter more as I perused the bookstore. The more I thought about it, the more sure I became that his totally innocent question was the key. When he asked me for the time, I was not thinking, *This guy is totally hitting on me. How obvious is he?* I just looked at my cell phone for the time and thought nothing more of it. His reading-list question had been equally innocent. I would have done the same thing if I had noticed someone with the reading list for a class I had to take. Once we started talking, we found we had a lot in common, which is when we started liking each other.

"Do you have the time?" was a perfect way to start talking to someone. If I remembered correctly, the last time I had needed to know the time, I hadn't searched out the hottest guy in the room. I had just turned to the person nearest to me.

It occurred to me that perhaps you could use any question to which you required an answer to start a conversation. The question didn't have to be time related.

I tried it out that very night.

Three years, too many dates and phone numbers to count, and an enormous amount of trial and error later, I finally feel I can say that I have cracked the mystery that tormented me for so long.

I've broken down everything I have learned and stuck it into this book. This is the book I wish I had owned when I realized that waiting around for the guy to make the first move was not going to work for me.

Whether you are interested in learning how to do what I dreamed of for so long—how to pick up guys successfully, sans props, and with virtually no risk to your ego—or you're just intrigued about what I learned, here's how to do it.

Quiz:
How Sassy Are You?

You're in a bar and see a Hot Guy across the room. You want to meet him, so you:

a. Get up and leave before you puke. This is much too scary to even think about.

b. Crumple up a piece of paper and throw it at his head.

c. Walk over to him, tap him on the shoulder, lift up your shirt, and flash him.

d. Catch his eye and smile while you stick out your chest a little more, but stay where you are. If he's into you, he'll figure out a way to talk to you. If he doesn't make the first move, he wasn't worth it anyway.

e. Pretend to check your voice mail as you meander in his direction. Once you're close, you'll ask him a question about what he thinks your friend should do about this new guy she's seeing.

Answer: e

2

how to
pick up
your hot guy

Opening

WHAT'S REALLY HAPPENING WHEN YOU HIT ON SOMEONE?

O**N** Valentine's Day my senior year of college, I went out on the town with four of my girlfriends. I soon discovered that National Singles Awareness Day was not the stay-at-home-and-wallow-in-noncoupledom pity party I thought everyone else thought it was. Instead, the day I thought all singles loathed was actually a very popular night for said singles to go out looking for a good time.

After a night of Valentine's Day debauchery, my friends and I sat down to grab some late-night sushi. We had just finished ordering when we noticed a macho-man guy using his best macho-man swagger to make his way over to our table. Because we were seated in the corner of the restaurant, we had the fortunate and amusing position of being able to watch him navigate the entire restaurant (no easy feat with the large number of chairs, tables, purses, jackets, and drunk patrons in his path). Because of this extended approach, we were able to observe that he was not able to place his arms flat against his sides because his biceps were so big, a fact that was advertised nicely by his too-tight T-shirt. I also noted that his hair had a fascinating tendency not to move at all, despite being long enough to hang in his eyes. I deduced that this was probably due to the super-plus bottle of extra-strength hair gel he had painstakingly but misguidedly used with the intention of looking hot.

Once arrived, he positioned himself at the head of our table. We all looked at him, wondering what this was about. Was he the restaurant manager and we were about to get some special service? Had we done something wrong? Was he someone's weird ex-boyfriend?

Instead, he proceeded to take a full twenty to thirty seconds of extremely awkward silence to undress each one of us with his eyes, making little grunts of approval (I think), when he found it appropriate. I found this extremely amusing, mostly because he so obviously thought he was rad. When he was finished with his visual undressing of us, he said (and I quote directly):

"I'm Dr. D. I'm worth a million dollars. You ladies are very nice to look at, but I bet you'd look even better with even less clothing . . . like, no clothing. Every other lady in here is watching me. Do you see them watching me? They all want to fuck me in the bathroom. Do you want to fuck me in the bathroom? I bet you do, because I'm worth a million dollars."

Awestruck at the stupidity of what he clearly thought was a charming speech, at first we were silent, which I'm sure

Dr. D. took as a good sign. Unfortunately for him, the silence was merely a pause. I think I snorted out loud first, and all my girlfriends immediately followed suit. We soon were all consumed with belly-shaking, tear-streaming, irrepressible, uncontrollable, snort-filled laughter. Given the slight intoxication we were all experiencing from our evening of fun stoking the hilarity, it took us a good ten minutes to calm down enough to eat.

Dr. D., who was not expecting this particular reaction, judging from the way his smile plummeted off his face and shattered on the beer-stained floor, managed (to his credit) to resume his swagger in a direction that took him far away from the pile of snorting girls he left in his wake. I presumed, once I was again capable of thought, that he was off to try his killer pitch on another group of single girls.

While I found Dr. D. extremely entertaining, he is relevant here because he is a good example of a truly awful pickup attempt.

What really happened was that Dr. D. let my friends and me know, in no uncertain terms, that he was interested in having sex with us (whether he was targeting just one of us or all of us was unclear). Unfortunately for Dr. D., whenever anyone from either sex can sense that they are being pursued, the following happens:

1. **We immediately place ourselves in a position of power.** After all, this person is pursuing ME, not vice versa. I can blow them off (by laughing at them, for example), and there are no consequences.

2. **Our pursuers become immediately less attractive to us.** Questions like "Why are they so desperate that

they feel like they have to come up and talk to me?" and "What's wrong with them?" are common.

3. **It is awkward.** The most frequent way I've seen a guy start a conversation with a girl is: "So, how are you doing tonight?" To which the ~~victim~~ girl (nine times out of ten) will reply with an icy version of "Fine." This type of direct interaction doesn't breed comfort for either party, and it doesn't lead into natural conversation. And yet I hear guys using those words on girls at least fifteen times every time I go out. It is such a common mistake, I don't think anyone even realizes that there are better ways to initiate conversation.

4. **It is boring.** You already know they're interested. The guys that we are attracted to are the ones who do not fall all over themselves or throw cheesy lines at us. The ones we like are the ones who are confident enough to give us a little bit of a chase, thereby assuring us that they are not desperate.

Basically, it boils down to the fact that the moment someone appears as if they are not interested, they become interesting. This works in reverse as well: the moment someone appears interested, they become uninteresting. However, going too far down the road of "uninterested" so that you look like a jerk to the person you like doesn't work that well, either. It's got to be just the right balance between interested and uninterested. This "just right" tactic is what I call the *Neutral Approach*.

Neutrality is a 5 on a scale of 1 to 10. It is the color beige, or that T-shirt I wear when I do laundry. It is that feeling that you could take it (the Hot Guy) or leave it. Translating this theory to a conversation with someone you are interested in is not to communicate in any way that you are sexually interested in that person. You don't show interest, but you don't show lack of interest. You could be talking to them, you could be talking to that other guy, or you could be talking to the guy over there. It doesn't matter to you because you're not "interested" in any of them.

This results in opening a communication channel between you and your target, but not the same communication channel that exists between two people who are sexually interested in each other. When sexual interest is apparent between strangers, awkward social interaction is almost always the result. The neutral interaction is entirely devoid of sexual interest. It breeds happiness on both sides because neither one is losing value in the other's eyes.

Neutral communication basically puts up a smoke screen that both parties can hide behind until they decide it's OK to show interest. It's a social tactic that creates natural, fun, and easy conversation.

In short, it's awesome.

How the Hell Do You Approach Someone Without Seeming Interested?

There are two situations in which it is socially acceptable to talk to someone you don't know. By the way, this initial contact is called *opening*, because you're opening a communication channel between you and the Hot Guy. These situations occur in daily life anywhere and anytime. They are both entirely neutral.

They are:

1. Where you have a need for information.
2. Where there is a current shared experience.

Here is a breakdown of each.

A NEED FOR INFORMATION

When I was riding the bus to Barnes & Noble and the guy behind me unintentionally started a conversation with me, he needed information from me: the time and then the lowdown on our shared class.

It is perfectly acceptable to approach a person you don't know when you need a piece of information. Asking for directions or the time is a good example of this. If I ask a guy for directions on the street, he's never going to assume that I'm interested, unless I incongruently show him I'm trying to get into his pants with my body language. If I am neutral, the interaction won't be awkward in the slightest. On the contrary, giving someone the time or helping someone get where they need to go is a pleasure. The only thing he is going to assume about me is that I felt him qualified to answer my question (i.e., he was wearing a watch).

Although asking someone for the time or directions nicely serves my purpose of demonstrating examples of needing information, unfortunately, they do not (normally) lead naturally into conversation. This is because his response will be either "Yeah, it's ten thirty-five" or "No, sorry." Questions with one-word answers do not an easy conversation make. In order for the conversation to continue (as the guy on the bus to Barnes & Noble did with me), there needs to be some other easy and obvious conversation topic as a natural follow-up.

Here is an example of a need for information that can lead into much more natural conversation and significant interactions than "Yep—it's eleven thirty."

Erin is in a boutique looking for a present for her boyfriend, so she finds herself browsing in the men's clothes section. She sees a tie that she thinks he might like, but she's worried that maybe it's a little intense for the office. There is a guy next to her also looking at ties. It is entirely natural for a confident girl such as her to ask the guy for his opinion: "Excuse me, I'm trying to pick out a tie as a present for my boyfriend. Do you think this one is OK for the office, or would he get laughed at?"

The guy might reply, "It's a cool tie. I'd wear it. Whether or not he'd get laughed at depends on the type of office, though."

At this point, Erin could just say, "Cool—thanks for your help." But it would also be completely natural for her to chat a little bit: "Yeah, that was my thought, too. He works in an architect's office, so being a little creative is fine, I think."

Both Erin and the guy will part having enjoyed some totally natural social contact with a stranger. There was no awkwardness, and neither suspected that the other was trying to get in his or her pants. Erin wasn't asking the guy about ties because she wanted to get to know him better; she has a boyfriend. She just needed information, and the guy qualified as someone who might have the answer.

It would be very different if Erin had said, "Hi—are you here to buy a tie?" because that would have shown an obvious interest in the guy and he would have thought, *Why does she care why I'm here?* The only possible reason she would ask that—and she's not employed by the store—would be that she wanted to start a conversation with him because she wanted to eventually have sex with him. Showing such overt interest would have lowered her value in his eyes and made the interaction awkward and uncomfortable.

In this scenario, Erin has a boyfriend. This made it 100 percent clear that her tone and body language were neutral. However, this conversation would have played out the same way if Erin had inserted "friend" into the conversation, instead of "boyfriend." She would have approached the situation with the same tone and body language as if she had said "boyfriend" because she would have conveyed no sexual interest in the guy looking at the ties. The only difference would be that the field would be open; the guy would have picked up that she was single. If he liked her, he would have conveyed interest, which Erin could then have reciprocated if she so chose.

If Erin's tone and manner are neutral, there is no guy alive who is going to think he is being hit on by someone asking for an opinion on a tie. It doesn't matter to the guy whether she needs advice about a present for her friend or for her boyfriend. Either way, she has a legitimate reason to have started talking to him, and he will be perfectly happy to chat.

To recap: where there is a need for information, it is totally and completely natural for two people who don't know each other to start talking. The girl has something she needs to know, and the guy looks like a good candidate for someone who can answer her question. As long as body language and tone are neutral, the receiver of the question is under no circumstances going to think that the person who asked the question is sexually interested in him.

The other situation where it is perfectly acceptable to talk to a guy you don't know is when there is something in your shared situation that is so interesting or so weird that it's unnatural NOT to say something about it. I discovered this nugget of information during my lunch break one day at work.

I was sitting on a bench in the park near my office, enjoying the warm spring day and eating my turkey sandwich. There was a Hot Guy sitting on the park bench next to mine, but I was at a loss for words. "Hey—it's a nice day, isn't it?" seemed beyond lame. Fortunately for me, nature intervened and I discovered a rather unreliable but effective way of starting a conversation with a cute stranger.

There was a pigeon that had happily discovered a forgotten french fry and was in a state of birdie rapture about six feet in front of me. Suddenly, an enormous squirrel came galloping down a neighboring tree and took a flying leap onto the back of the pigeon in what I can only assume was an attempt to steal the pigeon's booty. There was a brief but intense scuffle in which all I could see was fur and feathers, and then the pigeon managed to take flight with the squirrel on its back. The squirrel lasted about three seconds and then plopped back to earth from the height of about eight feet, french fry in hand (claw?). It seemed rather stunned, and I was about to get up and see if it was alive when it shook itself and staggered away to squat under its tree and eat its hard-won spoils.

The whole thing was extremely entertaining to watch, albeit slightly unbelievable, so I looked to the Hot Guy to see if he had also seen the scuffle. He was already looking in my direction, presumably for the same reason, and as soon as our eyes met, we started cracking up. This led to a series of half-finished sentences, much pointing at the scene of the squirrel attack, and wheezing because we were both laughing so hard:

"Did you see . . . ?"
"That squirrel!"
"Oh my god, I've never . . ."
"There are still feathers on the ground!"
" . . . squirrel print in the dust!"
" . . . fur . . . !"

After we were able to breathe normally again, we had a nice conversation. I found out he worked in the office above mine, he also enjoyed lattes, and we would meet for lunch the following week.

The natural human reaction when we see something unusual is to look around to verify that everyone else in the vicinity also saw the weird/funny/supernatural thing. It validates the situation for us and serves to assure us that we are not having a hallucinogenic episode. This validation creates a common moment between total strangers, and it's the social norm to acknowledge this moment.

The Hot Guy did not for a second assume I was hitting on him when I looked in his direction to check if he had also seen what I had just seen. He just assumed that I was looking for acknowledgment of an odd situation, as was he.

Using Neutral Openers to Meet Guys

To review, approaching a Hot Guy while showing an overt sexual interest in him does not work, at least not with any consistency. About 99 percent of the time, showing overt sexual interest will make him feel awkward, and it is very likely he'll remain aloof or even act like a jerk. Unless you're into social masochism, both of these reactions are exactly what you don't want. There are, however, certain situations in which it is socially acceptable to talk to a guy you don't know. These situations lead to natural interactions, and as long as your tone and body language match the neutral topic of conversation, no guy alive is going to suspect you are hitting on him.

You may be thinking, *This is great and all, but what am I supposed to do? Wait around for a psychotic squirrel to jump on a bird at the exact second I'm sitting next to a Hot Guy?*

Fortunately, this kind of patience is not necessary. The next bit of this chapter deals with creating situations that give you a shared situation to draw upon, something to ask, or both. In other words, I'm going to be talking about making up situations that suit your needs. Some of the glass-half-empty people out there will refer to this as lying. I see it as creative conversation-starting.

First, though, a note on neutral body language.

Body language communicates just as much as words do, if not more. If I am really and truly neutral toward the guy standing across the room, I am not going to look at him thirty-four times and try to make eye contact before I walk over. I would also have an alternate reason to be in his vicinity if I really and truly felt nothing about him. I would buy a drink, get a napkin, get a straw—anything that obviously explains my reason for being next to him (other than him) is fair game.

Not flirting before making contact is maybe the most difficult thing about these openers, and it was the hardest thing for me to conquer. If I'm interested in a guy, I'm going to look at him, right? I'm going to check him out, catch his eye, wink, flirt, and basically do whatever it takes until he notices me.

Unfortunately, this behavior is not at all congruent with my not caring whether I ever see him again. And since this is roughly the attitude you need to have while pulling off a neutral opener, it is imperative to have neutral body language.

Though it is difficult to ignore your targeted Hot Guy, the payoff is huge. Waiting for the guys I liked to come and talk to me rarely worked. Maybe for you it sometimes works. But that's the key word—*sometimes*. It is invaluable to me to get to choose the guy I get to talk to. Knowing that when I go and talk to him is going to be natural and smooth is amazing. I can talk to twenty guys a night if I want to, and not one will know that I'm hitting on him. The Hot Guy will just think I'm a cool, confident, not-interested-in-him-which-makes-me-hot chick.

A NEED FOR INFORMATION—CREATING A SITUATION

This is basically just making up some reason why you a) need to be near the guy you like, and b) need to talk to him so he can help you out.

Here is an example:

Mary is sitting with her friend in the corner of the bar, surveying the premises. She notices Hot Guy sitting at the bar with his friend. In order to talk to Hot Guy, Mary decides she is going to create a situation in which the Hot Guy will be the most likely candidate to give her the information she needs.

As Mary approaches the area where Hot Guy is sitting with his friend, she does not look at them, try to make eye contact, or even appear to notice them at all. She acts completely nonchalant and neutral as she walks up the bar to get another drink, casually slipping in beside the guys. While she waits for the bartender to get to her, she says to Hot Guy and his friend, "Hey, guys, can I ask you a question? My friend and I were just talking about this, and I'd like some guy opinions. She's been on one date with this new guy, and he said that on their second date he wants to take her to meet his friends. Don't you think that's a little intense— his taking her to meet his friends on the second date? She's not even sure she wants to date him and is uncomfortable meeting his friends if she decides he's not boyfriend material. What does it mean when a guy asks a girl to meet his friends?"

Mary is using the need for information as a pretext for talking to Hot Guy. She is not *appearing* to be interested in the guys at all (even though she is interested); she just needs a male opinion as fodder for her conversation with her friend. She is not saying things like "Where are you guys from?" or "How's it going?" or "Nice ass," all of which would be dead giveaways that she is interested in the Hot Guy. On the contrary, as far as Hot Guy and his friend are concerned, she's just a cool girl with a question that they can help her with. She has a perfectly acceptable reason for talking to them that doesn't convey interest in them at all. They don't feel like they are getting hit on. In fact, they will probably try to impress her to gain points with her.

Because Mary's question is pretty open-ended, Hot Guy and his friend ask her questions for clarification: "How did the first date go?" "Why doesn't she want to date him?" "Is he creepy?" The key thing is that a conversation has started—

a conversation that is incredibly easy to keep going. Dating is one of those topics that everyone has an opinion on, so after a couple of minutes, Mary and Hot Guy won't be strangers anymore. Their relationship will be as friendly as if they had been personally introduced by a mutual friend at a house party, if not even friendlier as a result of their slight history of shared conversation.

After the initial question has been discussed, Mary could then say (for example), "Thanks, guys—I appreciate the input. Where are you guys from?" It won't feel like she's hitting on them at this point, either. They have been talking for the last couple of minutes, and the next logical step is to find out more about one another. More personal questions that show interest are a natural extension of their current conversation.

The beauty of Mary's tactic is that it gave her a way to make the first move without Hot Guy realizing that he was being hit on. The curious (and cool) thing about this is that although the initial conversation was just based on a need for information, once that information has been exchanged, you no longer feel like strangers and it becomes quite normal to start asking questions like "Where are you from?" This then can lead into conversations that do convey a certain amount of interest. This works because once you are "in" neutrally, it will appear as though you became interested *after* he responded to your need for information. He'll walk away thinking about how smooth he was and how his suaveness totally picked up that hot girl from the bar.

Guys, as a whole (I'm generalizing, yes) and in my experience, love to feel as if they are in control. If we, as women, can give them the feeling of that power while getting to pick and choose our men, everyone wins.

A SHARED EXPERIENCE—CREATING A SITUATION

Here is an example of a shared experience, in a more applicable context than with daredevil squirrels:

Jenn is in college. She is in a lecture on environmental policy and happens to spy a Hot Guy sitting near the front of the lecture hall. The lecture ends, and Jenn subtly makes her way to the door at the exact moment that Hot Guy does. She does this without his noticing, so that as they leave the hall they are walking next to each other. She says to him quizzically, as if it had just struck her, "Wasn't that interesting what Dr. Jones was saying about the increasing popularity of bamboo? I didn't realize that so many people were aware of it." Hot Guy could respond in many ways: "Yeah, totally. I love this stuff. I think it's great that people are finally realizing that sustainability is the only intelligent solution." Or, "I didn't, either. You'd think we would have heard of it from the way he was talking, though." Either way, natural conversation can easily follow.

The common interest that Jenn cited—the fact that both she and Hot Guy were at the same lecture—makes it perfectly acceptable for Jenn to start a conversation with him. They've experienced the same thing, and she is talking about her perception of the lecture with the person nearest to her: Hot Guy. He does not know she planned to be there at the exact moment he left. She did not say, "Hey, hot stuff—want to grab a cup of coffee with me?" She was totally neutral with her topic of conversation. Based on her approach, there is no way he could know, at least not with any certainty, that she was interested in him.

However, although shared experiences clearly work if delivered neutrally, I'm not as big of a fan of them as I am of the need-for-information approaches. The reason is:

Everyone Uses Them.

This type of pickup line has been around as long as people have been trying to figure out how to get in one another's pants. Guys have been using situational stuff like, "Hey, it's a beautiful night, huh?" and "Isn't this wine great?" forever. They may recognize the tactic as something they would do, but then again, they may not. Very few people deliver these openers neutrally. A guy's body language often makes it clear that he is anything but neutral toward the girl to whom he's saying, "Wow, isn't this a great party?"

If you're going to use a shared experience as an opener, I recommend that you combine it with a need for information, which I talk about (conveniently) in the very next section.

A SHARED EXPERIENCE AND A NEED FOR INFORMATION— CREATING A SITUATION

This is much more powerful than just the shared experience opener alone.

Let's go back to Jenn's conversation with Hot Guy in the lecture hall. Instead of saying, "Wasn't that interesting what Dr. Jones was saying about the increased popularity of bamboo? I didn't realize so many people were aware of it," she could say, "Wasn't that interesting what Dr. Jones was saying about the increased popularity of bamboo? I didn't realize so many people were aware of it. . . . Can you help me with something? I didn't catch what percentage of businesses in California he said are now using bamboo as a wood alternative. Did you get that number?"

If, for the sake of argument, he did assume that she was totally hitting on him for the first part of the opener because he would have used the same line on a girl he liked, he would feel like an ass after she asked the question. She doesn't like him; she just needed an answer to her question. She totally negated the possibility that he might see through the situational comment by tacking the question onto the end of her opener.

The combination of a shared experience and a need for information makes for a very powerful but neutral opener, as well as one that will work extremely consistently. It stresses the common experience (they were in a lecture together) but gave Jenn a very plausible and completely neutral additional reason to be striking up a conversation with the Hot Guy.

The Neutral Opener—The Breakdown

Just to recap, so far I have talked about why neutral openers are so effective: they open a communication channel with a guy without conveying that you are interested in him, he gets to think he hit on you first and that's why you like him, and you got to pick the guy. It's a win-win situation.

Let's look at how the whole neutral-opener thing breaks down from start to finish. There are really five distinctly different parts (after locating the Hot Guy you're curious about):

1. **Get proximity** (neutrally, of course). You need to get near the guy to deliver your opener. Bellowing doesn't yield great results.

2. **Get into the right mental state.** If you want to open a guy by asking him his opinion on something you and your girlfriend were chatting about, you need to be completely in the mental space about whatever

you said you were chatting about. The same thing applies if you've made up the conversation you said you had with your girlfriend. Congruency is key. Otherwise, your question can come off as fake, and he may sense your lies.

3. **Deliver your opener.** Three rather clichéd but appropriate words are applicable here: *calm, cool, collected.*

4. **Follow-up conversation.** If he's shy, this takes more effort. If he's not, this will be surprisingly easy.

5. **Move into natural conversation.** Now it's on.

Here's a bit of detail on each step.

GET PROXIMITY

I think that proximity is the most important part of the opener.

As I've mentioned before, your body language is incredibly informative to the guy about what is really going on in your head. If I have no other obvious reason to be around Hot Guy other than Hot Guy himself, I will have conveyed my true purpose before I even started talking to him.

If I see a Hot Guy sitting alone in my relatively empty airplane, I would not, for example, make eyes at him for half an hour, then get up and take the seat next to him and start talking. I cannot by definition be neutral if he knows that I am there to talk to him before I even start talking. It's got to look as if I was there for something else, saw him, and then asked my question. In the airplane, I would wait for him to get up and walk around, not look at him and then contrive some reason for being in the same vicinity—for example, I am walking around, too. A neutral opener delivered then would remain completely neutral, and he would have no clue that I thought he was hot.

If I was in a bar and my targeted guy was sitting at the bar, I could need any number of things that would put me in the prime location, next to HIM: a napkin, a drink, or a pen to write down the number of the other Hot Guy I just talked to. I would be there for every reason other than the Hot Guy. He would have no idea what I was up to.

But what about those situations where there is no clear reason to get near Hot Guy?

Let's say you are in the reception area of your gym and Hot Guy is over by the door. He isn't close enough to the bulletin board to use that as a reason to be near him; in fact, there is nothing within ten feet of him besides the exit door. In this situation, you could pretend to check the messages on your cell phone and drift in his direction. Then, conveniently be "done" checking your messages when you are near enough to him to talk to him.

Cell phones are great props because checking your voice mail gives you a legitimate reason to be wandering almost anywhere. Even if, for example, your cell phone is busted because you dropped it in a glass of water, you can still *pretend* to use it. Everyone has them, so no one is going to think you are being weird with your itinerant message-checking. A further bonus is that they are not big enough to hurt yourself with—unlike, for example, a golf club.

There are, of course, more tricky situations in which proximity is a little more difficult. But have no fear: I've been in and thought of practically every situation you could get yourself into and have come up with a solution for all of them. They are listed in the appendix under "Even More Examples of Openers."

Essentially, this is just acting a part. You are playing the part of someone who is perplexed, say, about why guys need to be in control of the remote and have serious issues about letting anyone else channel surf. It helps (obviously) if this is already something that you are perplexed about. If, however, you find yourself not being perplexed about your dilemma at the appropriate moment, you're going to need to draw slightly on that second-grade acting class.

The first step to getting into the right mental state is to imagine how you would feel if your question *were* perplexing you right that second. You let your eyebrows draw together; you let a quizzical expression take over your face; you let the thought of why guys are such persistent remote-hoggers totally and completely dominate your world.

Then, because you already have proximity, you turn to the guys nearest to you (your preselected targets) and ask, "Hey, guys, tell me something. Why is it that guys always have to have total and complete domination of the remote?"

Once you start talking to them about the subject that was so completely occupying you that you absolutely *had* to ask the person next to you, you won't have to act anymore. The conversation will flow, and you can just be yourself. You will only need to act for about twenty seconds, which is just about long enough to deliver your opener successfully.

The point of being in the right mental state is that if you are not totally in the mental place you need to be in to make your body language congruent with your words, the whole thing may come off as being a little fake. The guys might assume either that you are hiding something (I had one guy ask me if I was dealing drugs and could he buy some?) or that you yourself are a fake person. Obviously, neither of these is the goal when opening (i.e., starting a conversation with) the Hot Guy. However, if you can put yourself in the mental place where your question really is something that is bothering you and you really don't feel as if you can wait one more second to get an answer, everything will align. Your body language, your tone, and your words will all be congruent. When all these things come together, there is not a guy alive who won't try to answer your question.

I've found that putting myself into the required mental state while I have proximity works best. After much testing, I have discovered that when I try doing it before I start getting proximity, I tend to focus so much on the subject at hand either I forget what I'm supposed to be doing or I run into things—neither of which is conducive to my goal. I think it is safe to say that there are people out there who can both hold a train of thought and not lose their focus, so my way certainly isn't the only way. That said, the great thing about getting into your mental state while you have proximity is that your facial expression will change as you start wondering about the why behind your question. It will appear to anyone watching you that you just thought of something. This just makes you appear even more congruent, which is never a bad thing.

DELIVER YOUR OPENER

Bars can be noisy, coffee shops can be too quiet, and outdoor places can make it hard to hear because of the wind and ambient noise.

It took me a bit of time to learn this, but it is important to adjust the volume of your voice according to the social situation. It also helps tremendously to speak clearly and slowly, as in: Don't. Rush. Your. Words. You want Hot Guy to understand you the first time you say something and not have to ask you to repeat what you said.

Proper delivery of your opener falls into the same category as public speaking. Speaking too quickly not only is hard to understand, it conveys nervousness and undermines your message. Why would you be so nervous about just asking a guy for some information if that was truly all you were doing?

If you're the type of person who gets nervous speaking to people or nervous about saying "lines," practice in front of the mirror and listen to yourself talk. This may cause your roommates to question your sanity, but the more times you say your opener, the more natural and less nervous you'll be. Remember, Hot Guy has no idea that you are hitting on him. You're just a cool chick with a question.

FOLLOW-UP CONVERSATION

The openers I have used as examples so far can be taken lots of places after the guy has had a chance to respond to the question.

Sometimes, the answers that he gives will be sufficiently interesting or detailed that the conversation will flow naturally. Other times, the guy may be shy, quiet, or just plain antisocial. His reasons behind how he responds are varied and totally unpredictable: he may be in awe that this cool girl is talking to HIM, his dog may have died that day, or maybe you look like his sister. You have no way of knowing why he's not being a chatterbox, but for whatever reason, he's not.

Because you can't tell what the guy is going to be like before you talk to him, it's a good idea to have an idea of where you could take the conversation after his initial reply.

For example, let's go back to how Mary opened Hot Guy in the bar at the beginning of the previous chapter. If Hot Guy had responded with an "Um," Mary would need something to keep the conversation going. She could have said, "Do you think it makes a difference that they're girlfriends or guy friends that he wants to introduce her to?" By her second question, he should have gotten back his wits if he lost them temporarily, or gotten back his confidence if he was a little shy.

In my experience, it very rarely takes more than about thirty seconds for an interaction to get to the point where you are just chatting naturally and easily. If it is taking longer than that, he's got issues, or something was a little off in your approach. Move on and try again.

MOVE INTO NATURAL CONVERSATION

After about thirty seconds of conversation, it is natural to start chatting normally as if you had just been introduced to each other by a mutual friend. For example, instead of assuming that you are desperately trying to pick him up when you say, "So, do you live around here?" he will assume he must have played his cards right because you, the Hot Girl, went from not interested in him to interested in him after he laid down his killer advice as to why guys hog the remote.

I have included more information on moving into natural conversation in the Post-Opening section, under "This Is a Girl I Want to Get to Know" and "The Importance of Building Rapport."

I hope I've persuaded you that neutral approaches are a golden way to meet guys.

The next part serves as an easy introduction into the world of picking up guys, if it's not something you have done before. And judging from 99 percent of the girls I've talked to, it's something not many girls have tried.

This part is also what I use for myself if I'm having one of those nights where my self-esteem bottoms out. You know the nights I'm talking about: they happen after those days when I have PMS times ten, I can't seem to do anything right at work, and I spill coffee on my white pants. On those days, I have to ease myself back into the groove to remind myself I can do it. Going all out when I'm not feeling it seldom gets me anywhere.

5 Techniques to Build Skills and Confidence

I've broken this down into five levels. When I use this for myself, I start with the next level up from where I feel confident.

The five levels are designed so that they each work to some extent as an opener. Level one is the easiest; level five is the most difficult, but also the most effective.

You will probably meet a lot of guys while climbing the difficulty ladder just by practicing the lower levels. Stick to it and move up a level when you feel ready to tackle the challenge.

LEVEL 1

This is the opposite of what you want to actually do in a real pickup attempt, because you're letting the guy know you like him by looking at him. However, when you need a confidence boost, it fits in very nicely.

Just make eye contact with a guy you're curious about. You don't have to get proximity; you don't have to worry about opening him; you don't even have to say anything. If you're feeling especially brave, you can smile at him. He'll know that you are interested, but that's fine: your aim at this level is just to get used to making contact with a guy you like. Depending on the social situation, probably about eight times out of ten nothing will happen. If you are in a bar, he may get the hint and have the courage to come over to you maybe one time in five. If you are in a grocery store, he may just think you're looking at someone over his shoulder and maybe only one guy in ten will approach you. But at least you're doing something that works sometimes, and you don't have to lay yourself on the line. You are not risking rejection because you know it hardly ever works anyway, so if he doesn't come over and talk to you, it's nothing personal.

If you are shyer than shy, this is a great place to start.

LEVEL 2

Just get proximity. That's it. The goal of this level is to build up the courage to get near Hot Guy. If you remember my experience, you don't want to get so near that you knock him off his chair. But you do want to be near enough that if he has the courage to start a conversation, he'll be able to.

Use your cell phone. Pretend that you are checking your messages (or actually check your messages) and meander pretty much anywhere. There is no way this will look like a deliberate approach. If you are in the bar and he is in the bar, it's easy to get near him—get a drink, a napkin, whatever.

If he's not at the bar, there's usually a route that can lead to near where he is. You can go look at songs on the jukebox, watch the pool game, go to the bathroom, or go outside for some air.

The idea here is just to get comfortable with the experience of deliberately getting near the guy and to practice doing it in such a way that he has no idea you are doing anything deliberate. More often than you would expect, he'll talk to you anyway: you're near him, you're hot. If not, again, it's nothing personal. Maybe he was still too intimidated, even though you made it easy by getting near him. Getting comfortable with positioning yourself near your target is imperative in opening. Again, I think positioning is half the battle.

LEVEL 3

Get proximity to Hot Guy and then ask him a question that definitely does not lead to a conversation—for example, "Do you know what time it is?" Because this is merely a simple request for information, there is no sexual pressure and he is definitely not going to assume you're hitting on him—especially because as soon as he gives you the time, you're going to say "Thanks!" and then walk away. That's it. Again, you may be surprised how often he will try to continue the conversation.

Just remember not to be wearing your watch.

LEVEL 4

Get proximity to Hot Guy and ask him a question that leads to a conversation, but make it overtly clear that you have no interest in him by mentioning your "boyfriend."

Go into any store and get proximity with a guy. He doesn't have to be cute; you're just practicing. Ask him, "Can I ask you something? I'm trying to pick out something for my boyfriend's birthday. Do you think this sweater/DVD/MP3 player/watch is cool?" There is no guy on earth who will think that a girl is hitting on him if she mentions her boyfriend in the first breath, so you are guaranteed that this interaction will be neutral. This is great practice for experiencing how a neutral interaction should go.

Unfortunately, you've also guaranteed that the interaction is not going to go very far, but that's not a problem because the aim at this point is just to get comfortable with opening.

LEVEL 5

OK—you're ready! Do an approach like you did in level four, but don't mention the "boyfriend," instead replacing it with "friend." The interaction is neutral and therefore could very easily lead into a conversation. If you have worked through the other levels and are comfortable with them, by now you should have the skills to carry this off.

I give you a ton of examples for every situation I could think of in the next part, as well as going into how you can come up with great openers of your own.

14 Examples of Openers

The examples I have listed here all follow the same basic formula. This formula is completely based on using a neutral approach: first you get proximity, then you get into the right mental place, then you deliver the opener, then you follow up.

The openers listed here and the ones in the appendix are all ones I have used myself, so you can be assured that they do indeed work.

You can play with the actual words in the openers and make them your own. After all, it's a lot easier to get into the frame of wondering something enough to want to know a guy's opinion on it if you are actually, genuinely wondering about that thing. I give you these as a guideline. Feel free to add to, delete from, or re-create them as you see fit.

You'll note that for most of the guy's responses to these openers, I've put "blah blah blah." This is because I want to emphasize that it doesn't matter what the guy says in response. Your objective when you open Hot Guy is to have an opener and two to three follow-up things you can say, regardless of what Hot Guy says back to you. If he says something that is easy to respond to, then by all means follow his conversational thread. But for the cases where he doesn't say anything useful that can be used to continue the conversation, you don't want to stall and get stuck saying, "Uh . . ." Because you have no idea whether or not the guy will be a conversationalist before you approach him, it is necessary to have two or three things already planned ahead of time.

Here is an example of what I mean. In the first conversation, I've put "blah blah blah" for his answers. In the second, I've filled in the responses for what the guy might say. You'll note that in both cases, the opener and follow-up items are exactly the same. I've done this to stress the point that if he's unresponsive, you can keep going with the conversation because you've already got something to say all planned out. Hopefully, he'll open up after the first or second follow-up item.

▶ James Bond Opener 1

YOU: My friends and I are having a debate about who was the best James Bond. It's split pretty evenly between Sean Connery, Daniel Craig, and Pierce Brosnan. Who's right?

HIM: Blah blah blah.

YOU: Well, which Bond movie was the best?

HIM: Blah blah blah.

YOU: Seriously? Now I'm interested—your opinions are so different from/the same as (depending on what he said) mine! What are your top five movies of all time?

▶ James Bond Opener 2

YOU: My friends and I are having a debate about who was the best James Bond. It's split pretty evenly between Sean Connery, Daniel Craig, and Pierce Brosnan. Who's right?

HIM: Um . . . I guess I feel equally neutral about all of them.

YOU: Well, which Bond movie was the best?

HIM: Um . . . the last Daniel Craig one was pretty good, actionwise. I guess I'd say that one.

YOU: Seriously? Now I'm interested—your opinion is the same as mine! What are your top five movies of all time?

See what I mean? His response didn't leave any room for further conversation on the Pierce versus Sean versus Daniel debate. By following up with a similar thread that stayed within the same topic, he finally responded. The third thing you said introduced yet a new thread that invited much further discussion and kept the conversation going.

One more thing: I've only included a choice few openers in this part just to give you some ideas. There are a lot more examples in the appendix. During my trial-and-error years, I kept thinking of situations where I was convinced that there was no possible way to open a guy. Then I'd think of a potential solution and test it. I've tried to list every possible situation in the appendix so that if you find yourself thinking, *There's no way I could talk to that guy I pass in the subway every morning*, like I did, you'll be pleasantly surprised to find out there is.

This part is not meant to be read through, but merely used as a reference.

Enjoy at your leisure!

I like bars. There are a lot of guys all in one place, and if it's Friday or Saturday night, they're very likely to be single. No one is in a hurry to be somewhere else, and it is the social norm for people to be chatting about random stuff. Bars are also often fairly noisy, so that only people in your immediate vicinity can hear what you're saying. Happily, this means you can use the same openers several times on different groups of guys. The next few openers are good for bar use.

▶ Gym Opener

YOU: Hey, guys, can you tell me something? How come guys grunt in the gym? I was traumatized today by this guy who was grunting so loudly, you could hear him in the reception area. What's the deal with that? Why do guys do that?

THEM: Blah blah blah.

YOU: Women don't feel the need to grunt, even though they're exerting themselves—we're both human, so it must be biologically possible for guys not to grunt.

THEM: Blah blah blah.

YOU: OK, I concede that sometimes women grunt—like in tennis. But even then, it's not really that loud, it's more like a squeak than a grunt. So you guys are grunters, huh?

THEM: Blah blah blah.

YOU: Hmm. You look like grunters.

THEM: Blah blah blah.

Angelina Jolie Opener

YOU: Can I ask you guys something?

THEM: Blah blah blah.

YOU: Do guys think that Angelina Jolie is hot?

(Note: Notice that the question is not "Do YOU think that Angelina Jolie is hot?" By asking if "guys" in general think she's hot, you're emphasizing that it's not the opinion of any particular guy you're after; it's the general male population's opinion. The latter is neutral; the former is not.)

THEM: Blah blah blah.

YOU: You know, it's funny—My girlfriend and I have discovered that most girls think she's gorgeous, but a lot of guys don't think she's that hot. Isn't that weird?

THEM: Blah blah blah.

YOU: What about Julia Roberts? Do you think her smile is too wide? A lot of my guy friends seem to think so.

(Note: Here it's OK to ask about his opinion, because you're in the follow-up portion of the conversation. After the initial opener and his response, it's fine to express a bit of interest.)

THEM: Blah blah blah.

YOU: I went and saw [insert movie title here] last week. Have you guys seen that movie yet?

(Note: This is a fantastic follow-up question that can pretty much be tacked on to the end of any opener. People always have opinions about movies, so it's an easy way to keep the conversation going.)

Remote Control Opener

YOU: Hey, guys, tell me something: What is the deal with guys and the remote? I was over at my girlfriend's house earlier with a bunch of guys to watch the game. Every time the commercials came on, they freaked out if we tried to change the channel. What is the deal with that?

THEM: Blah blah blah.

YOU: What is it, exactly, they think girls are going to do with the remote?

THEM: Blah blah blah.

YOU: How do you expect girls to learn how to use your crazy-ass remote system if you guys are always hanging on to it? How good would you get programming the TiVo if girls always did it for you?

THEM: Blah blah blah.

YOU: We have this guy friend who bought TiVo a year ago, and we've hardly seen him since. What's the deal with that? It's like he's found a spouse.

THEM: Blah blah blah.

Try these when you're not in a bar:

At the Grocery or Liquor Store

YOU: Excuse me—can I ask you a question?

HIM: Blah blah blah.

YOU: Thanks. I'm going to my first poker game tonight, and I want to bring something cool along with me so they'll invite me back—what's something you've seen at poker games besides chips and salsa?

HIM: Blah blah blah.

YOU: Beer, huh? What's a step up from Bud Light? These guys are Bud Light guys, but I want to expand their horizons.

HIM: Blah blah blah.

YOU: OK—I'll get them some [insert beer brand here]. Would you believe I've spent the whole afternoon trying to remember the order of hands, like flush, straight, and all that. Do you have any tips for how to win?

HIM: Blah blah blah.

▶ In a Coffee Shop

[Go outside and pretend to (or actually) talk on your phone. Come back in and sit down near the guy you want to meet.]

YOU: Excuse me—can I ask you something? I was just talking to my friend on the phone, and she's kind of upset. She met this guy a few weeks ago, and they've been on a couple of dates. He just left her this voice mail saying, "I had fun on Tuesday. See you around." What does "See you around" translate to, in guyspeak?

HIM: Hmmm. Well, I know when I say it, it means I hope I see the girl again, but I don't feel the need to set up another date then and there.

YOU: Well, in this case do you think the guy means that he doesn't want to see her again or that he does?

HIM: It's not a complete write-off, but if he had really been into her, he would have set up another date.

YOU: Huh. I'll have to pass that on. They had a great first date at that new restaurant on Main—have you been there?

Alternatively, if you're in a situation where making fun of gender stereotypes isn't socially acceptable, these openers will work. Remember, I've listed more example openers in the appendix, and many of them are not strictly "As a guy, what do you think"—based.

▶ At the Bookstore

YOU: Excuse me—can I ask you a question? I'm trying to buy a present for my guy friend. Do you think it's messed up to buy someone that book *Dating for Dummies?*

HIM: Blah blah blah.

YOU: Yeah, he's a really cool guy, but he always comes on too strong and scares the girls off. We all try to tell him, but he doesn't really listen.

HIM: Blah blah blah.

YOU: What about if I bought him a gadget? Do you know which gadgets are especially hot at the moment?

HIM: Blah blah blah.

YOU: Wow, you seem like you know a lot about it—do you work in a tech field?

▶ On the Street

YOU: Excuse me—do you know if there's a bookstore around here?

HIM: Blah blah blah.

YOU: Can you believe I've been living around here for over a year and I still don't know where the bookstore is? I love bookstores, but I've been too busy to go find the local one. Even now, I'm not buying a book for me to read—I'm getting a present for a friend. Can I ask you, as a guy, do you think it's messed up to buy someone that book *Dating for Dummies*?

HIM: Blah blah blah.

[Then you can just run the bookstore opener. I put in this example to show you how you can combine openers and use them in lots of different situations by running one opener into another.]

Anywhere

[Have a twenty-dollar bill with you.]

YOU: Can I tell you a secret?

HIM: Sure. . . .

YOU: I just found twenty dollars on the street. I looked all around and I couldn't see anyone who could have dropped it. Do you think it's OK for me to keep it?

HIM: (laughing) Well, if you didn't see anyone drop it, I guess it's your lucky day.

YOU: I just feel kind of bad, you know? I feel like I should do something special with it, like . . . buy ten ice cream cones or something. What do you think?

HIM: There's always the ninety-nine-cent store. You could get twenty somethings there.

YOU: Great idea! So, what are you doing [today/tonight, depending] that brings you here?

While traveling (for business or pleasure), many of the same openers you would use at home will work, especially when you're in a club or bar. However, here are few examples of some situations where it would be useful to know how to talk to a foreign Hot Guy. If the Hot Guy is a business traveler, he'll probably be very willing to chat—traveling for work by yourself (as I'm sure many of you know) can get pretty lonely!

At the Hotel Bar: X Games Opener

(Note: The X Games have international versions, such as Latin X Games, European X Games, Asian X Tour—so you can substitute in a more geographically accurate version if you'd like.)

YOU: Can I ask you guys something? You know the X Games, right? Well, my girlfriends and I were talking this afternoon, and it was brought up that if you mess up in the X Games, you don't usually get a second chance. Do these guys just have enormous balls and just train knowing it could be their last trick. or do they use harnesses and safety nets and stuff?

HIM: Blah blah blah.

YOU: Really? I have to admit their hotness level went down a bit—it was pretty hot to think that they were so hard-core that they didn't need safety nets, but I guess it makes sense. Speaking of which, we were also talking about the definition of hard-core. How would you define hard-core—like in a sport sense?

HIM: Blah blah blah.

YOU: Interesting. So can you be hard-core about, say, badminton?

At the Hotel Bar: Restaurant Opener

(Note: This one works really well in places known for their food [i.e., Mexico, Italy, Japan]. You can extend the conversation by inquiring after genuine and/or local fare and not the fake touristy restaurants.)

YOU: Excuse me, can I ask you a question? Do you know of any great [insert your favorite restaurant type here, i.e., Italian, Mexican, Japanese] around here? I've got a massive craving.

HIM: Blah blah blah.

YOU: Awesome, thanks. What about good touristy gift shops that really exemplify [insert city name]? I need a memento for my sister.

HIM: Blah blah blah.

YOU: Oh, that's a great idea. What brings you here? Are you traveling on business like me?

HIM: Blah blah blah.

At the Museum

YOU: I know I should be thinking about [the art/the museum/the show/etc.], but I can't help thinking about something I just saw. . . . I just saw these two girls down on the street, and they passed each other, and one of them said something to the other as they passed. Then, the first girl—who looked really pissed off—took a twenty-dollar bill out of her purse, wadded it up, and threw it at the other girl. It was the weirdest thing I've ever seen. Is that normal?

HIM: Blah blah blah.

YOU: Would you ever throw money at someone?

HIM: Blah blah blah.

On the Train

YOU: Excuse me, do you have the time?

HIM: Blah blah blah.

YOU: I think I'll just make it. . . . I need to be at [insert destination here] by seven thirty. Do you happen to know the fastest way to get there?

HIM: Blah blah blah.

YOU: Great, thanks. It's nice that the train is so convenient. It's not like that everywhere. Is this your usual train?

HIM: Blah blah blah.

Some Ideas for Making Up Your Own Openers

▶ *"Help Us Clear Up Our [insert descriptor here] Argument"*

You could be having any random argument with your friends and need an outside opinion to determine who is right. Guy-related situations, or at least situations that are interesting to guys, are convenient; "Guys? Who makes better shoes—Christian Louboutin or Jimmy Choo?" is unlikely to cut it, but the following examples will work just fine:

> YOU: Guys—help me out here. I'm arguing with my friends, and they're saying that Terminator was a crappy movie and that Arnie was lame. Help me beat some sanity into them. They're completely missing the point, right? (Or pick any movie that you thought was good but that some girls don't like.)

> YOU: OK, guys—help me out here. My guy friends (you can point to them) are saying that the only activities that count as hard-core are activities where you can really get hurt, like rock climbing or skydiving or boxing or something. But I think you can be hard-core about something else like marathon running or even tennis if you took it seriously enough. Who is right, do you think?

▶ **What Should I Do About . . .**

Here you just think of a scenario, real or imagined, that could benefit from some male input.

> YOU: Guys, I'm wondering if you can help me out with

something here. One of my friends met this guy a week ago, he said he would call her, and they exchanged numbers. Should she call him, or is he just not calling because he isn't into her?

Why Does This Work?

Why do these openers work so well compared to just saying "Hi" or complimenting his sneaker choice?

Because you are completely absorbed in your own reality.

Something is happening in your own life that you want clarification on, advice on, or an explanation for, and it just so happens that a guy would be well qualified to give you that advice. The more strongly you are in your reality, the more obvious it is to the guy that there is no way you could be hitting on him.

After one of these openers, if a male friend came up to Hot Guy and said, "Dude, that girl was totally hitting on you," he would honestly reply, "No, man, she wasn't hitting on me. She has a guy friend who got into [insert situation here], and she needed some advice on it. She's just about to call him. . . ." or "Negative—she was having an argument with her friends, and she just wanted some extra opinions on something." Even if he suspects that you might have been hitting on him, there is a perfectly acceptable alternative explanation for your approach, and that smoke screen is what makes the interaction comfortable.

Which opener you use is usually just a question of sensitivity to the social situation. If you're in a club or a bar, some of the more chatty, amusing openers are better, because they are the most congruent with people out for a night of fun in a bar.

But if you are in a park or waiting to tee off on a golf course, something a little more sedate is clearly called for. If you are outside where guys are not necessarily expecting to be spoken to by anyone, you want to pitch your opener for that type of situation—in other words, you'll probably want to tone it down a bit and stick to the more "So sorry for interrupting you, but I have a question that desperately needs answering" openers.

The key, as always, is the neutral opener. Since you do not convey any sexual interest in Hot Guy, it disarms any suspicion that you might be hitting on him and leads to a nice, natural interaction. This can lead to Date #1 if he's as cool as you thought he might be.

The "Good Guys" Are Everywhere

Another thing I have discovered is that there are a lot more good-looking, cool, intelligent, funny, sensitive guys out there than I originally thought.

It appears—and I'm guesstimating here—that roughly 10 percent of the guys out on any given night are the guys that have the confidence to approach girls. These are the guys whose egos are so big and oozing with "I'm the shit" that it's difficult to get within ten feet of them without getting splashed. These guys are the players of the world. They're also, on the whole, total jerks and therefore completely undatable.

Another 20 percent (or so) of the guys out on any given night are not compatible with the majority of the female population. Perhaps their relationship with personal hygiene is on the rocks, perhaps their criminal records have line items, or perhaps they're socially maladjusted and need more time to develop their personalities. Perhaps they're exploding with issues. Whatever the problem is, they fall at the opposite end of the spectrum from the players but are equally undatable.

The remaining 70 percent (or thereabouts) are the cute, fun, normal, cool guys. You know all those great guy friends everyone you know has? These are those guys. You just don't ever meet them because of one simple reason:

From a guy's perspective, approaching girls is a daunting task. (Shocking, I know.)

These cute, fun, normal, cool guys have tried a few times to approach girls but were shot down because they didn't know what they were doing and were unfortunately mistaken for being card-carrying members of the undatable team. Not being gluttons for ego-trouncing by flat-out rejection, fake phone numbers, and being laughed at, they have basically given up.

Why do these cute, fun, normal, cool, "great guy friend" guys have a hard time with girls? They are not losers. They are not dorks. They are not freaks. Most of them are not even shy. Unfortunately for them, however, they do lack the knowledge needed to successfully breach that great divide that exists between members of the opposite sex when wanting to hook up is on the table.

Ultimately, what made them candidates for rejection was their obvious approach. The four-step process mentioned earlier (see page 43) kicked into gear the second they started talking, which resulted in an immediate loss of credibility, attractiveness, and power in the interaction.

This 70 percent is going to remain girlfriendless unless initiative is taken.

Drinking and Pickup = Alcohol-Induced Eyewear

I've noticed a common misconception with pickup: liquid courage (i.e., alcohol) is a great way to boost confidence. This is *so* not true.

Heavy drinking and pickup are never best friends, or even friends at all. At best, they are acquaintances who get along only when drinking is on a very short leash. Personal experience has taught me that when I'm on the prowl, it's a much better idea to keep the boozing to a minimum. Why?

Beer goggles.

When you drink to the point of letting down your guard and increasing your confidence, your perception of those around you will change as well: every guy will look like a Hot Guy. Wasting a whole night getting cozy with a dude who would normally rate a 4—but falls into the Hot Guy category because of your alcohol-induced eyewear—is not the ideal situation.

Since the whole point is to meet a guy you *actually* think is Hot, putting on beer goggles is about the most counterproductive thing you can do.

51 Places to Meet Guys

All of the following are excellent places to meet new people. Some of them are more friendly for just hanging out, and some do double duty and expand your horizons by teaching you something new.

1. **Line Dancing** (Lots of talking. Lots of laughing because hardly anyone knows what they're doing. No-pressure environment. Lots of fun.)

2. **Salsa Clubs** (Usually the salsa club will offer an inexpensive, informal class before the actual club opens. If you don't know how to salsa, these classes are great. Also, you'll make some new friends. Lots of single guys looking for fun girls to salsa with go to these clubs.)

3. **Sailing Classes/Regattas** (Excellent places to mingle with a lot of outdoorsy, fun-loving single guys and make new friends. Knowing how to sail is not required, but it does help. You can always ask for tips from the Hot Guys!)

4. **Soccer/Rugby/Cricket matches** (Everyone goes to watch, including the Hot Guy friends of the Hot Guy players. While you're enjoying the athletic prowess, you can talk to the Hot Guy friends.)

5. **Croquet** (This slightly antiquated sport is gaining more traction in the younger crowds and is a lot of fun to play. Check out clubs in your area and join in!)

6. **Group Coed Golf/Tennis Lessons** (Both sports lessons are perfect places to meet Hot Guys. Both are fun to play, are very active, and, if you make new friends, open up the weekend tournament circuit to you.)

7. **Scuba Diving** (The instructors are usually Hot Guys, and Hot Adventurous Guys love scuba diving. Plus, once you know how, it opens up a whole new realm of activity on vacation, or, if you live near water, a whole new group of fun, awesome people to hang with on weekend boat trips. When I got certified, there were no less than eight single guys in my class.)

8. **Beach Volleyball Tournaments** (Lots of attractive people play, and lots of attractive people go to watch. Very enjoyable.)

9. **Running/Cycling Clubs** (Get some exercise and meet a ton of new people. Every running and/or cycling club I've ever come across has been at least 60 percent male . . . and they're definitely Hot.)

10. **Triathlon Clubs** (If you haven't done a triathlon before, try one. The club provides training support and mentorship, and you're surrounded by perfect bodies.)

11. **Team in Training** (Or some other training club. If you're interested in running a marathon or doing a walk for charity or entering a bike race, these are great places to meet new people. They're almost always coed, and you can always suggest a little extra training with your chosen Hot Guy on the side.)

12. **Masters Swimming** (A swimming club with a coach. Usually they meet four or five times a week, but you can come as often as you'd like. A great way to stay in shape and meet some Hot Swimmer Guys.)

13. **Yoga Studios** (Take a class or sign up for their events. Either way, yoga studios are filled with beautiful, fit, and usually really nice people. Hot Guys galore.)

14. **Coed Gym Class** (For example: kickboxing. Get a great workout and meet some very fit Hot Guys.)

15. **Rock Climbing** (Never have you seen so many fit, half-naked guys. It's a mecca for the Hot Guy outdoorsy types. This applies to both outdoor rock-climbing clubs or competitions, and indoor gyms.)

16. **Ice-skating** (When you fall, ask the Hot Guy for a hand up. The cocoa/coffee stand is also an excellent place to hang.)

17. **Rollerskating** (Check out the seventies- and eighties-themed nights for a good time. They're packed with fun-loving, cool people.)

18. **Skiing/Snowboarding** (If you venture away from your group for a bit, you'll find yourself in the fortunate position of needing a partner to ride the chairlift with you. That single Hot Guy would do nicely, no?)

19. **Painting Class** (I signed up for a painting class after a bad breakup a couple of years ago and was shocked to discover that of the ten students, nine were single and seven were Hot Guys. Tap this resource, people.)

20. **Sculpture Class** (Same idea as painting class, plus you get to pretend you're in *Ghost*.)

21. **Photography Class** (Improve your skills, or learn something new. When they make you partner up for a project, ask the Hot Guy to pair up with you.)

22. **Writing Class** (Improve your writing skills and join Hot Guy's writing group. Suggest grabbing a beer or coffee after class with the group and you're home free.)

23. **Cooking Class** (Learn a lifelong skill and meet some Hot Guy foodies.)

24. **Coffee Shops** (They're great places for musing, reading, writing, or just enjoying some awesome soy nonfat latte action. Usually, at least four Hot Guys are present at all times.)

25. **The Apple Store** (Everyone loves a new iPod. Go and check out the new gadgets and absorb the awesomeness of all the Hot Nerds.)

26. **Adventure Supply Stores** (REI is a good example. The guys that work there are typically Hot Guys, and so are the customers. You can't go wrong. Plus, they all want to help you figure out what you need for your next adventure. It's a perfect conversation starter.)

27. **Office Supply Stores** (Lots to look at. Everyone goes there.)

28. **Bookstores** (Books are the perfect excuse to wander into the vicinity of your targeted Hot Guy.)

29. **Airports/Train Stations** (Hot Guys travel, too. While you're waiting for your plane/train, pass the time by indulging your curiosity about the Hot Guy next to you.)

30. **Airplanes/Trains** (Same as above, except make use of the social areas of the plane/train—the bar [in larger planes], viewing deck [on a train], or bathroom lines.)

31. **Weight Watchers** (Even if you don't need to lose any weight, Weight Watchers teaches the basic tenets of good eating and living healthily. The meetings are great places to make new friends and expand your social circle.)

32. **Co-op (and Regular) Grocery Stores** (Everyone goes to regular grocery stores, and again there's lots to look at. Co-op grocery stores can be even better—some require you to work three or four hours per week, although others don't. If you work, you meet a ton of like-minded, hip people. If you don't, just

doing your shopping there will expose you to a pre-selected segment of society that you'll already like!)

33. **Whole Foods/Trader Joe's** (Favorites among the young, urban, and hip, both are great places to meet Hot Guys. All those guys you've been eyeing in your yoga class go to Whole Foods, guaranteed.)

34. **The counter or community table at a restaurant** (Go alone—good for meeting other singles, and you can avoid that whole sitting-by-yourself-at-a-two-person-table thing.)

35. **Volunteering at your local children's literary/home-work help center** (My favorite are the 826 National centers [visit www.826national.org to see what I'm talking about]. Look for one in your area. In my experience, these centers attract the most interesting, fun, hip people you've met in a long time.)

36. **Political rallies** (Stand up for what you believe in with some signage, a homemade T-shirt, some peaceful protesting, and some like-minded Hot Guys.)

37. **Political fund-raisers** (Same idea as the political rallies, except you usually get to dress up and wear killer heels.)

38. **Environmental Meetings** (Help out a cause and meet some eco-friendly Hot Guys at the same time.)

39. **Beach/Lake/Park Cleanup Events** (Hang outside for five hours, do something awesome for your community, and be exposed to a ton of Hot Guys.)

40. **Organized Hikes** (Organizations like the Sierra Club and stores such as REI, in addition to local clubs, all organize hikes on a pretty regular basis. Get some exercise and meet some Hot Guys.)

41. **Spoken-Word Events** (Often friendly, open atmospheres that facilitate interesting discussion. Many have refreshments available. Single Hot Guys will be in attendance.)

42. **Open-Mic Nights** (You might have to sit through some pretty bad performances, but these events can occasionally be really good. Everyone's got to start somewhere, and often the performer's friends will come to support, so the crowd has the potential to be full of Hot Guys.)

43. **Library Functions** (You'd be surprised at how many local libraries host movie screenings and mixers. Check the local calendar and utilize this free social outlet.)

44. **Art Openings** (Not only are openings excellent places to meet Hot Guys, art is also the perfect excuse to strike up random conversations with strangers: "I love this painting. It makes me think of a deep sea vent. Do you know if that's what the artist was going for?")

45. **Museum Functions** (Take in a little culture or history, and meet some Hot Guys at the same time.)

46. **Wrap Parties** (Happy atmosphere, open bar.)

47. **At the Bar or After-Party at a Concert** (Everyone's happy and revved up from the music, and you know you at least have one thing in common.)

48. **Wine/Beer Bars** (Quieter, more friendly atmospheres than their crazier cousins.)

49. **Book Clubs** (Although these are traditionally mostly women, you can always expand your social circle and meet their single Hot Guy friends.)

50. **Alumni Events** (Especially for college. If you went to

a larger school, you won't know the vast majority of the people in attendance. Plus, you've already got one thing in common.)

51. **Your Own Club** (If there's not a club in your area for what you're interested in, start one. At the very least, you'll make new friends. At the most, all of your members will be Hot Guys.)

17 Party Ideas to Make Them Come To You

For all of the party ideas listed below, encourage your friends to bring someone outside of their normal social circle. The idea is to get a mixed group larger than your normal group of friends so that you can all meet new people. All those "great guy friends" that everyone has? This is the perfect opportunity to meet them.

1. **Bring-a-Friend Party** (Have each of your friends, both male and female, bring at least one single friend with them. Couples are allowed, but only if they bring a single friend. Because there are so many singles there, your single friend will WANT to come, as opposed to grudgingly accepting your invitation.)

2. **13 Party** (Friends bring pictures of themselves when they were thirteen years old and wear an outfit as close as possible to what they wore when they were that age. The best costume wins.)

3. **Graffiti Party** (Everyone wears a white T-shirt they don't care about. You provide the markers. Everyone tags each other and you all end up with a killer souvenir.)

4. **Bad Christmas Sweater Party** (Go to your local thrift store and find the most hideous Christmas sweater you can find or take an old moth-eaten sweater and bedazzle it with Christmas decorations. Offer a cash prize for the worst sweater.)

5. **Cross-dressing Underwear Party** (Girls wear guys' underwear. Guys wear girls' underwear.)

6. **Rock Star Party** (Everyone dresses up as their favorite rock star. Have everyone bring the mixings for their favorite drink.)

7. **Sports Party** (Everyone dresses in the uniform for their favorite sport. Encourage Speedo and wrestling uniforms for some instant hilarity.)

8. **Color Theme Party** (Pick a color and require that everyone attending be wearing that color, head to toe. Bonus points for picking a less popular color, such as orange.)

9. **Stereotype Party** (Everyone dresses up as a stereotype. For example: ditzy blonde, gold-digging wife, rock star, investment banker, cowboy, supermodel. The best and most easily identifiable stereotype wins.)

10. **Hidden Talents Party** (Everyone signs up for a two-minute slot to perform or show off a hidden talent. Examples include bird calling, smoothie making, and bubble-letter writing.)

11. **Clothes Swap Party** (Everyone in attendance must wear something he or she no longer wants. The idea is to swap what you're wearing with someone who is wearing something you like. Encourages random conversations with people you don't know as well

as some fun nakedness. Encourage attendance by friends of friends, whom you don't know.

12. **Halloween Costume Swap Party** (Everyone wears an old Halloween costume and swapping ensues. An excellent way to take care of your Halloween costume early.)

13. **Jell-O Party** (Everyone dresses up as a color of Jell-O, and Jell-O shots are offered in abundance.)

14. **Beer-Tasting Party** (Everyone brings a six-pack of his or her favorite beer, or the most random beer they can find. Google "beer tasting" and create a beer-tasting cheat sheet for everyone listing the different facets on which beer is judged. Hand out shot glasses for the tasting process so that the beer doesn't go too fast. The best beer wins.)

15. **Wine-Tasting Party** (Similar to the Beer-Tasting Party—everyone brings a bottle of his or her favorite wine, or the most random wine they can find. Print out cheat sheets and provide shot glasses for the tasting. The best wine wins.)

16. **Dessert Party** (Everyone brings a favorite dessert, whether it's homemade or store-bought. The best one wins.)

17. **Potluck Dinner Party** (Save yourself the headache of making a dinner party happen by just having each of your guests bring a dish. Divvy up entree, dessert, appetizer, and drink assignments.)

More ideas for both where to meet guys and party ideas are listed on my website: www.screwcupidthebook.com.

Crap Advice: *Girls shouldn't EVER make the first move.*

Why Is It Crap? The main argument for this ideology is that supposedly guys don't like girls who make the first move. This is simply not true. There is the occasional exception, but in general, guys LOVE when girls make the first move. It takes the pressure off them.

• SECTION 2 •
Post-Opening

Thıs is the part of the equation that gets you from initiating the talking to having a full-blown conversation.

There are several parts to post-opening: *This Is a Girl I Want to Get to Know*—What You Want Him to Think, The Importance of Building Rapport, and Closing the Deal and Getting to Date #1. Depending on the vibe you have with Hot Guy, you can skip some or all of the parts before screening. However, these parts are good to know when you have a target who is not very forthcoming with his friendly vibe.

This Is a Girl I Want to Get to Know—
What You Want Him to Think

This comes directly after the opener. It consists of interesting or entertaining filler that piques Hot Guy's interest so that he thinks, *This is a girl I want to get to know.* This is the period that gives you a chance to define who you are, without too much intensity.

The first five minutes of the conversation, including the opener, make up the unconscious testing period for most people. Let's say a guy hits on YOU: if he can get through those five minutes without saying anything that sets off your alarm bells, he is 90 percent of the way there. When the situation is reversed, and you are the one talking to Hot Guy, you want the same thing to happen.

You sail through these five minutes and emerge triumphant on the other side by showing Hot Guy that you are a normal, fun, and interesting person because you have fun and interesting things to say. You do not quiz him on his attributes. You do not try to get to know him. You just talk and entertain him for a couple of minutes. There is no deep conversation, because your sole purpose is to keep the conversation going with funny, interesting fluff. You are not going to be saying anything that expresses interest in Hot Guy, so you are not going to come across as needy, and because of this, your neutral status remains clear throughout this period.

Here is an example of what I mean:

"So, I was reading this article online today about this fish pond in Vermont where, for two weeks out of the year, there is a law that states that the people who live there are allowed to get their guns out and shoot the fish in the pond. This strikes me as a little weird on several levels: first off, they had to make this law because these people wanted to shoot fish the other fifty weeks of the year? Plus, isn't shooting a fish kind of counterproductive? I mean, they're pretty small—shooting them with a shotgun would turn them into shark bait, not dinner. And this is all beside the fact that shooting a gun into a lake is dangerous. They said that the gunshot wounds around this lake increase, like, fifty percent during this two-week period because the bullets ricochet off the water, and people end up shooting themselves and people on the other side of the lake because of the deflection."

The things you say can be stuff about you, stuff about the news, or something you saw. It should last for about two to three minutes, so that if your opener lasts two or three minutes, you'll have hit the five-minute mark by the end.

After that, you should have a pretty good idea of whether or not Hot Guy likes you. If he doesn't seem interested, try throwing in a couple more minutes of fun, entertaining stories, or move on to establishing a rapport (the next part).

Caveat: If the vibe seems right—in other words, if, right after the opener, he's obviously totally into you—you can skip this part entirely. If the conversation seems like it can move into personal questions without it being weird or awkward, it's OK to do so.

You can also recycle the stories that you use: Hot Guy isn't going to know. I've put a few of my personal favorites below so that you can get a further idea of what I mean:

"The funniest thing happened to me earlier today. I was in my office, minding my own business, and all of a sudden I heard this woofing noise by the door. I looked up, and there was the most enormous dog I've ever seen: his head was ABOVE the level of the door handle. He was huge. He also looked like a wolf, and—not that I'm scared of dogs—but *damn*. This one was pretty intense. So while I'm sitting there trying to figure out what to do, the dog took a liking to my door handle and was kind of gnawing on it. Then I heard this lady in the lobby calling, "Snowflake! Snoooooooowflaaaaaake," and the monster turns around and gallops toward her voice, leaving a waterfall of drool on my door handle. I saw her walk by a couple of minutes later, and, I'm not kidding, this woman was about eighty years old and maybe five feet tall. The dog came up to her shoulder. It was crazy."

"You know those squirrels that live around here? How huge they are? Well, I was sitting on the grass outside work today during lunch, chatting to my friend. I was holding my sandwich in my right hand and kind of gesturing to prove a point, as you do. While I was talking, my friend started cracking up because this ENORMOUS squirrel had waddled over to us and had his little paws on my sandwich! This, of course, surprised me quite a bit, and instead of having a tug-of-war with the squirrel, I ended up dropping the sandwich and relinquishing my lunch to the little fatty. It was ridiculous. He wasn't even scared of me!"

"The most embarrassing thing happened to me yesterday at the gym. I don't know if I'll be able to show my face there again. I was just finishing my run on the treadmill—do you know that really funny walk-glide thing you do when you get off the treadmill and get on the nonmoving floor? So, I'm trying really hard not to look like a dork while walking to the exit doing my walk-glide. No one was looking at me and laughing, so I felt good about it. However, I saw this really hot girl and guy handing out flyers near the door and was so distracted, I failed to see this stand they had up advertising 'Ab-Nite' or whatever it was and glided directly into the sign—like, into it so that I knocked the whole thing over and tripped myself in the process. It was quality. To make matters worse, when I tried to get up, I was still in gliding mode and a little off balance, so I had a really hard time trying to make the poster stand up by itself again. I eventually managed it and laughed it off (as you have to in a situation like that) and attempted to leave as quickly as possible. Once again, I wasn't looking where I was going, and I ended up smacking into the glass door. I'm sure they all thought I had major motor skill issues. So I push the door that says 'PULL' in huge letters, figure that out, pull it open, and leave. I hope I made someone's day—it was probably hysterical to watch."

"Snowboarding? Let me tell you a little story about the last time I went snowboarding. So, my cousin and I were marooned together at a semi–family reunion last Christmas. He's some champion snowboarder or something and so we decided to head to the slopes so he could show me the ropes. We also decided it would be a really good idea to have a couple of shots at the bar upon arrival. This, while fun, was probably not the greatest idea we've ever had. So we got to the top of the mountain and attempted to make our way down. I've boarded maybe three times in my whole life and am not what you would call skilled—I'm a skier normally. And even though he was really good, we'd had enough that our balance and general awareness, two things that come in handy while trying to snowboard, tended not to be so in tune. So I was boarding, upright (which I was proud of), and I started picking up speed. This is when I remembered a little too late that I don't know how to stop without falling. I'm very rapidly approaching the lift line and those orange net divider things, and he's yelling "Use your edge!" and I'm thinking, *Yeah, right! I'm going about twenty miles per hour!* So I decide to just fall backward and hope for the best. The best turned out to be tumbling ass over heels into the lift line and taking out five of the hottest guys I've ever seen, along with part of the orange fence thing. Luckily for me, the hot guys found it humorous—and my cousin and I were laughing so hard, it took us about half an hour to calm down enough to try again. It was awesome."

"Field hockey, huh? I have a great story about hockey. So, I was in high school. My team was practicing on the intramural field that all the teams in the whole school shared. On this particular day, conservatively, about eighty percent of my school was watching our practice: waiting for the field after us, taking a break from their practice, or just enjoying the day. So, when my friend passed me the ball, all eyes were on me. And then when I got past the goalie, who had run to quarter field like a dork, all eyes were REALLY on me. I was thinking, *I'm so cool—I'm totally going to score this fantastic goal in front of all these people—I'm so awesome!!* What I don't realize is that I'm running really, really fast—too fast, in fact, to stop in time before the goal. So, I end up running full speed into the back of the goal, knocking the whole goal over and tangling myself up in the net so much that it took them about ten minutes to extricate me. Best of all, some jackass with a video camera caught the whole thing on tape and played it the next morning on the student news. It was my crowning moment—good stuff, no?"

The Importance of Building Rapport

Building rapport is the part of the conversation where you make him like you and you express some interest in him.

He already thinks you are cool from your two to three minutes of entertaining fluff, but in order for him to really like you, you've got to make a connection with him. Up to this point, you have not tried to make an attempt to get to know him further; your stories served the purpose of making him laugh and demonstrating that you're a cool, functioning girl. No deeper connection besides "We laughed together" has yet been made. This is the part where you do try to make a connection.

You start to build your link with resident Hot Guy by getting into the kinds of conversations that allow you to exchange enough personal information that he sees you as more than just a cool girl and starts to see you as someone he'd like to hang out with. Depending on how comfortable you feel or how quickly you feel Hot Guy is going to open up, you can bring in more intense conversation, or you can stick with lighter conversation.

If you haven't already, you will figure out whether or not this is a guy you want to see again.

I offer some guidelines here, but there aren't really any rules for this part—it is totally based on you and your personal preferences for small talk. I trust that you know how to make small talk that leads you to the conversations that build a connection with the person you're talking to. You just do your thing and let your true colors shine through.

Rapport questions can be a little tricky. Your aim is to get to know him a little bit—but caution should be taken about the types of questions you ask and how you ask them. You don't want to sound like an FBI agent interviewing a felon.

For example, asking him what he does for a living will set off most guys' "gold-digging" alarm bells.

An example of a good rapport question is to tell a story about something you've done (or your friend has done, or you saw done on TV) recently and ask him if he's ever done that: "I went rollerblading the other day, ended up on this huge hill and caught air, and I surprised myself by not eating it—it's been a while. Have you ever done that?" The "Have you ever done that?" is the key component because you're now asking him things about himself and expressing interest in him. You're basically just being chatty: anything that pops into your head is cool to use.

Part of this portion of post-opening is showing some overt interest in him. Questions like, "Do you live around here?"

"How long have you lived around here?" "I've always wanted to go skydiving (or rock climbing, or whatever)—have you ever done that?" are fair game. Once you've asked a few questions like that, if you want to introduce something deeper, you can easily mix it in.

Deeper conversation topics can be brought up on the sly (preferable), or they can be brought up in a more intense manner (not preferable).

For example, asking Hot Guy, "What's your religion?" or "Where do you stand on abortion?" has the strong possibility of coming off sounding more than slightly confrontational. Instead, you could broach those topics by saying "My friends and I were having this really interesting conversation earlier today—we were trying to decide how we determine the difference between right and wrong. What would your answer be?" This is a religion question/screen. If he says, "I look to the Bible/Torah/Koran for inspiration whenever I have a moral question like that," he's going to fall into the religious category.

The abortion question can be broached in a similar fashion, if you feel like diving into that: "My friends and I were having this really intense conversation earlier today about abortion. We were talking about the why behind the debate and where people get their stances. What do you think?" It is easy enough at this point to ask him where he stands and why. It still qualifies as a direct, intense question, but since you mentioned that you were talking about it earlier with your buddies, he's not going to be as on guard as if you had said, "Are you one of those people who believes that choosing to have an abortion makes the person a baby killer?"

These deeper topics are more intellectual than your average day-to-day conversation, and he'll appreciate that you are more interesting than the airhead next to you.

To sum up, building rapport is that natural conversation you have when you are trying to get to know someone enough so that you feel, and he feels, that the connection forged when you are done talking is sufficient to want to continue the great conversation at a later date (i.e., Date #1).

Closing the Deal and Getting to Date #1

So you opened Hot Guy at the bar, and you've been chatting with him for maybe twenty minutes: you've demonstrated your value, and you've built the rapport. He's pretty cool and he seems to be enjoying the conversation, but the idiot hasn't made any move to ask for your number yet. You could continue talking to him if you're having a good time, but let's say for argument's sake that you're itching to move on to the next guy to meet your quota of meeting ten guys tonight. This translates to "I need to get back to my friends." However, you'd like to continue things on Date #1 with the current Hot Guy—what now?

Well, asking for his number is an option, but it's not the best option you have. The downside of doing this before he has made it obvious he's into your hot self is this: it lowers your value in his eyes. By asking for his number first, you have effectively revealed that you are into him before he has communicated to you that he'd like to hang out. No good.

Option two is to suggest that you exchange numbers. This is marginally better because exchanging numbers means that you're both letting on that you want to see each other again. However, phones are lame: whether or not you admit it, we've all spent a considerable amount of time waiting for the damn phone to ring. Your long-lost cousin calls you, your grandmother calls you, a telemarketer calls you—but he doesn't call, and suddenly your day sucks.

If you've exchanged numbers, things get infinitely more complicated because we all know that the first person who calls loses. So it becomes this totally lame game in which you obey the *Swingers* mantra of waiting three days to call, but when you do, he's not there, so you leave a voice mail. And then he waits a day or two to call back so he doesn't look desperate and leaves you a voice mail. And then you have to wait to return his voice mail so that you don't look desperate, and before you know it, a week has passed, you can barely remember him, and you both drop it.

I find this game-playing excruciating. It irritates me, both on the it-is-impossibly-annoying hand and on the I-feel-like-a-loser-because-I'm-waiting-for-the-phone-to-ring hand. Because of this, I've banned phones from my dating vocabulary.

The tried, true, and totally infallibly effective method for setting up Date #1 is this:

Set up the date there and then.

It cuts out all the games—every single one. There's no BS to deal with, and it weeds out the flakers immediately because they'll just hem and haw and not find a day to meet you. It is way easier to flake on calling someone than it is to flake on an actual meeting. No one likes standing someone else up: it makes them feel mean. Instead, the potential flakers will make it obvious that their schedule is MUCH too full this week, so why don't they get your number to set up something next week? The good ones will suggest a meeting in a few days' time.

There are two ways to broach the topic of setting up a date.

1. Say your friends are waiting and you should go. Then wait for him to make the next move.
2. Say, "I've really enjoyed this—what's your schedule like this week?"

Try the first, and if that doesn't work, try the second. Here's the full breakdown of both:

The first way is just to say, "I've had such a good time talking to you, but I'm completely neglecting my friends." Then, just hang around. About 80 percent of the time, he'll ask for your number. If this happens, you can say, "Actually, I'm not that big on phones, but what's your schedule like this week?" His Hot Guy heart will leap for joy, because now he knows for sure that you want to meet him again and you aren't going to be just another girl who gives out her number but doesn't return calls. Just agree on a time and a place to meet and swap numbers just in case there is a change in schedule: "Awesome. Let's swap numbers just in case, but unless I talk to you on the phone, I'll see you there at eight on Thursday!"

And that's all there is to it: you can put a big fat check mark in the box for Date #1 with Hot Guy. There's no bipolar manic elation followed by crash landing every time the phone rings and it isn't him. There is no voice-mail drama. And, best of all, there are no games.

If he doesn't ask for your number, he is probably part of that 20 percent of guys who are too shy or nervous to ask for your number. This 20 percent consists of the guys who've been burned so often, they don't even try anymore. The supershy/nonsocial guys also fall into this category. All these guys are awesome, but their self-esteem is a little lower than the average bear's, so they don't know that they're awesome. They're also often not that familiar with the whole dating thing, so they don't know the etiquette with what's OK and what's not. Your option, if he falls into this 20 percent, is to help him out. For example, you could say, "I've had such a good time chatting with you, but I need to go. What's your schedule like this week?" and set up a meeting from there.

I feel that reality, although harsh, is a necessary topic here. The never-talked-about fourth option is that there is a slim possibility that even though he has liked the conversation and he has enjoyed your company, he doesn't want to see you again.

Just like you screen him, he's screening you. Maybe he's Jewish and only dates Jewish girls, and you're not. Maybe he just broke up with his girlfriend two weeks ago, and chatting with you really cheered him up, but he is in that I-need-to-just-be-alone phase right now.

If he does not seem keen on meeting again, you can just say, "Well, it's been a pleasure meeting you!" and move on. No harm done, except perhaps a very slightly bruised ego on your part. If this happens, don't stress. Now that you can talk to any guy you want, finding another one who will be into meeting you for a first date is a snap.

QUIZ:
Are You a Pickup Master?

You see a Hot Guy standing in a group composed of other Hot Guys and one Hot Girl. To meet him, you:

a. Walk up to the group and punch her in the face. If she's not conscious, she can't get in your way.

b. Go to the bar and pound five shots of tequila. You'll never have the courage to talk to him otherwise.

c. Hover creepily three feet away from the group, stick out your boobs, and wink lasciviously at the Hot Guy while flipping off the girl.

d. Wait until a lull in their conversation, politely interrupt, and ask them why guys always hog the remote, making sure you pay as much attention to the girl as you do the guys.

e. Leave. There's no way to talk to him.

Answer: d

· SECTION 3 ·
Refining Your Game

THESE are the tips and tactics that fall under the more advanced category. Now that I've explained opening, having a conversation, and closing, the more advanced tactics will make sense.

Wings: Picking Up Hot Guys with Your Friends

You may notice that the examples I listed earlier and the further examples in the appendix can all be used when you're by yourself—you don't need to have a friend with you. That said, having a friend or wing with you can make for an awesome girls'-night-out activity.

PICKING UP GUYS—WITH YOUR GIRLFRIENDS

Let's say you're in a bar and you're going to use the "Do guys think Angelina Jolie is hot?" opener. If you were using it to open guys by yourself, you would just say, "Hey guys— can you help me out with something? My friend and I were arguing about Angelina Jolie. She says that guys think she's hot, but all my guy friends say her lips are too big. Who's right? Is she hot or not?" You can follow up with "How about Julia Roberts? Is her mouth too wide? All my guy friends say that, too."

But you could just as easily have your girlfriend with you.

This has several benefits:

1. **Proximity.** With a wing or buddy, it is much easier to get proximity naturally. If you are by yourself and the guys you want to open happen to start a conversation among themselves just as you approach, it can make opening a little tricky. You can't just stand around by yourself and wait for their conversation to be over, unless they are situated in a place (like at the bar) where you could be doing something else. If they're in the middle of the room, you have a real challenge to get proximity to them naturally without looking weird.

   However, if you have a friend with you, you could stand together and chat wherever the guys are. This will look completely natural. All you have to do is wait out their conversation and then open them. As long as you do this subtly, they won't have a clue that you are both in their vicinity purely for the reason of talking to them. They'll just think that you and your friend found that space three feet away from them to be a convenient place to hang out. You have a lot more leeway with a friend than you do by yourself, especially when opening larger groups of guys.

2. **Acting is easier when you've got a wing.** Another added benefit of being two instead of one while hitting on guys is that it can make getting into the right mental state much easier. If you and your friend get proximity and then have your "discussion" about Angelina Jolie while you are within earshot of the Hot Guys, it becomes very natural

to turn to them and state your case: "Hey, guys—my friend and I were just talking about Angelina Jolie. SHE (point to your friend) says guys think she's hot, but all my guy friends say her lips are too big. Who's right?" The guys will jump on the opportunity to help out not one but two lovely ladies who need their opinion.

3. **There is someone else to carry the conversation.** If you're opening more than one guy, having your girlfriend there is great because you can both add to the conversation. This makes it that much easier to keep the conversation going if one of you should forget what you were about to say next. It is also a lot of fun to share the adrenaline rush of picking up guys with someone else.

4. **She can "take one for the team."** If you've opened two guys, you probably opened them because you thought one of them qualified as a Hot Guy. But then again, maybe both are Hot Guys and you don't care which you talk to. If this second case happens, rock on. And email me when, where, and what night of the week this happened to you at sam@screwcupidthebook.com. My personal experience has shown me that it's more likely than not I'll have more of an attraction to one of the guys than the other.

In a perfect world, when you approach Hot Guy and his not-hot friend, the Hot Guy would always be the one who showed interest in you. Unfortunately, in reality it is perfectly possible for the other guy to find you attractive, and Hot Guy will back off out of respect for his friend. Obviously, this is frustrating because you really want to be talking to Hot Guy, but his friend keeps hogging the conversation. If you have a friend there, you can agree in advance that one of you will occupy the not-hot guy while you talk to the one you like. You can take turns doing this for each other so that, over the course of the evening, you've both had plenty of opportunities to meet cool (and Hot) guys.

And there you have it—four good reasons to have a buddy when you go hunting.

I've found that going out with my girlfriends to pick up guys is a blast. I don't know about you, but before I figured this stuff out, "girls' night out" fell into one of two scenarios. In the first, which rarely occurred, we would split up to talk to separate guys, and each of us might actually have a chance. In the second scenario, there would be this unspoken pact to hang with the girls—and only the girls. If this was the situation, I always felt like I was committing some major faux pas if I left the group to talk to a guy. Sure, there were nights I had a great time with just the girls and only wanted to spend time with them, but marooning myself in a large group of very unapproachable chicks every time we went out wasn't high on my agenda. It really bothered me because I felt like the chief reason we spent so much time "out" was to meet guys. And how was I supposed to meet guys if I got guilt-tripped every time I left the pack?

Fortunately for my conscience, once I figured out the secret of how to pick up guys, "girls' night out" suddenly became a night where we could spend the whole night together (awesome) and have a blast picking up guys together (equally awesome). The buddy system was the perfect answer.

But, as with all brilliant answers, there were a couple of pitfalls I learned very quickly to avoid, and so I've devised the following ground rules for picking up guys with your girlfriends.

As a girl who has girlfriends, I've noticed that in groups of girls, even close friends, it is fairly common (OK, very common) for there to be competition over guys. This is because it is pretty unusual for a cool guy to come into a group of friends' social circle. So when a great guy does come along, competition can run rampant, friendships end, everyone ends up taking sides, and chaos ensues.

The underlying problem is this: the common belief is that there are not enough cool guys to go around. Decent guys are seen as a scarce resource, and wherever there is a scarce resource, there will be more than one hot girl who wants that resource. If you and your girlfriends meet one or two cool new guys a month, competition is a natural reaction.

But what if you met ten great new guys a week? Suddenly, it doesn't seem that important to be fighting over one specific guy: there are tons more where he came from. The abundance mentality is entirely and totally necessary for making it work with a female buddy. When you think that there are lots of guys out there, taking one for the team seems like an option rather than a lack of self-respect. Cooperating seems possible, instead of feeling like you're giving up a guy to your friend. The strategies and techniques I outline here really work. It's very realistic to meet ten new guys a week just by going out a couple of nights. Scarcity of decent guys doesn't ever need to be an issue.

So, the number one rule for a female buddy is to cooperate. That means that you take one for the team so that your friend can talk to the guy she digs, and then she'll take one for the team when you see Mr. Right Now sitting with his not-so-attractive friend. You occupy the nontarget while she works her magic, and she will do the same for you.

Cooperating also means not trying to score points off each other or cut each other down when you're talking to guys. Instead, build each other up. Going out with a friend instantly validates YOU: you're clearly a social, well-adjusted, cool person if you have a friend with you. Let's say your friend is telling a story about how she bungee jumped off a hundred-foot bridge. Rather than saying, "Well, when I was skydiving in New Zealand last year . . . ," instead you could say "That's so like you—you're so cool. Isn't she great?" The good vibes will also make you both feel good, even if the guys turn out to be dorks.

It's also very (very) useful to make up codes for certain situations. The situations I'm talking about are those times when discussing logistics is impossible, but you still want to let each other know what's going on and what you're feeling about the situation. I've laid out a few of the most common situations where having secret codes is extraordinarily useful:

- You're not so into the guy you're talking to, but your friend seems to be interested in him. Does she want to swap?
- You've had enough. Is your friend ready to ditch these guys?
- You really like your guy. Is your friend happy to let you go off so that you can both talk to your guys one-on-one?

My friend Audrey and I used to bring up the topic of going to the beach that weekend if we wanted to ditch the guys we were talking to. If we wanted to swap, one of us would say she felt like a gin and tonic, and if one of us wanted to be alone with the guy, we would ask to borrow ten dollars for "parking money."

As you gain more experience meeting guys together, you will get a feel for the best way to communicate. Just make sure it's not obvious to the guys: that can produce some majorly awkward conversation.

PICKING UP GUYS—WITH YOUR GUY FRIENDS

It can also be really fun picking up guys with a male friend. How, you ask?

I've got a couple of male friends I go out with on a regular basis, with smashing results. Having a male wing is about as neutral as you can get. How can Hot Guy think you're hitting on him if you didn't even start the conversation?

The best way for this to work is for you and your friend to separate. You can stay at your table, at the bar, or with your other friends as your guy friend wanders off and pretends to be looking around the bar. Guys are always doing this while looking for cute girls, so this is totally natural. You've already told him which Hot Guys you want him to talk to for you, so he just continues to check out the room as he gets proximity to the Hot Guys.

Your friend can open the Hot Guys with just about anything: it is very easy for a guy to talk to other guys in a bar. In other places, what he opens the Hot Guys with will have to be altered depending on the situation, but it can be just as easy. In a bar, he can say, "There are some hot chicks out tonight. I was just over at (name some other club) and it's pretty quiet, but this is so much better—good landscape, huh?" I have found that 100 percent of guys will respond to this 100 percent of the time. They won't think your friend is hitting on them because he just mentioned girls. And your friend is bringing up a universal guy subject: chicks. Other universal guy subjects like "the game last night," cars, and golf are all fair game. Whatever your friend feels like talking about is fine. All he's doing is opening the communication channel for you.

Then it's simply a matter of you walking fairly near to where he is, apparently on the way to the bathroom or wherever. Your guy friend calls out "Hey, Michelle (or whatever your name happens to be)!" and then brings you into the conversation by saying something like, "I was just talking to these guys about some of the bars around here. What's that bar over on Fourth Street—the one with the pool table?" Or he could say something just as neutral that brings you into the conversation without it being forced. He can introduce you as his friend so that the other guys feel comfortable hitting on you. From there, it is easy enough for you all to chat. Once you are settled into an easy conversation, your male friend can excuse himself to go to the bathroom and leave you to get to know your new Hot Guy friends better.

Why would any guy do this for you?

1. It's really fun planning this stuff out. It feels very undercover spy.
2. You can do the same thing for him. Girls can talk to other girls just as easily as guys can talk to other guys. I'll go so far as to say that it's probably even

easier. He can pick out girls he likes, you can pick out guys you like, and you'll both go home with lots of numbers. It's great.

What Happens When He Doesn't Respond? Combining Openers

Your first and only opener should work swimmingly in about half of the situations you'll find yourself in. The conversation will start easily, things will go smoothly, and everything will be golden.

However, in some situations, just one opener will not be enough to make a great conversation. Maybe the guy is shy. Maybe he's never heard of Angelina Jolie. Maybe the bar is loud and he didn't hear most of your first opener. Maybe the opener you chose didn't strike a chord with him and he's not vibing with you yet. These things are clearly not in your control, which is why I suggest having backup plans in case you run into one of these guys who does not immediately fall all over himself to talk to you.

This backup plan is to use more than one opener, back-to-back. This gives the guy you are talking to more time to do one of the following (depending on the situation): recover and figure out something to say back to you (if he's shy), pick up on the second opener because the first one blew right past him, or hear what you said because it's so loud. The openers you choose depend on the situation. If you're in a sports bar, the more entertaining openers will work great. If you're at your company fund-raiser, something more sedate may be in order.

Here's an example of what I mean:

YOU: Guys. Tell me something. Do guys think Angelina Jolie is hot? My friend and I were just talking about her and she says that guys think she's hot, but all my guy friends say that her lips are too big. [Opener #1]

HIM: Er . . . she's OK. [A nonresponse.]

YOU: And what about Julia Roberts? Is her mouth too wide? [Follow-up]

HIM: Er . . . she's OK. [Another nonresponse. Time to go into Opener #2)

YOU: Hey—can you explain something else to me? How come guys always grunt in the gym? Women don't do it, so why do guys need to? [Opener #2]

HIM: Heh-heh. Yeah, a lot of guys grunt. [A response!]

YOU: Are you a grunter? I bet you are. You look like grunter.

HIM: Nooo! I don't grunt. Or at least not normally—although if I'm doing a really heavy set, then I'll maybe grunt a little bit. [Now he's into it. Congrats! The conversation is on!]

YOU: What does it sound like? Like 'Uhhhh' or is it more 'GGrrrrr'?

HIM: Heh-heh-heh. I guess it's more like an 'nnnnggggggaaahhh!'

YOU: I was right! I knew you were a grunter. Which gym do you go to?

HIM: I go to the private gym down on Sixth Street. How about you?

YOU: I go to that huge one on Tenth.

him: What are you training for—anything in particular? [Etc.]

The guy in this situation didn't respond to the question about Angelina or about Julia. Maybe he just needed a bit of warming up; maybe he didn't get it—whatever the reason, he responded to the second opener, which was inserted flawlessly. There was no pause in the conversation: you just kept right on going. And it worked! If Opener #2 hadn't worked, you could have inserted another opener to see if that broke the ice. It is good to have two or three openers planned in advance, just in case the guy is slow to respond.

Combining openers also works for situations in which it is not the social norm to approach someone (unlike in a bar, coffee shop, grocery store, or whatever). Let's say, for example, that your target Hot Guy is on the beach. He is on his towel, reading a book. He also has thirty feet of unoccupied sand around him in every direction, making a subtle approach totally impossible. What do you do?

If you just walk up and say, "Hi," he's probably going to think you're a stalker. However, if you instead run a very simple opener before you run your real opener (i.e., combine your openers) you can very easily attain natural, easy conversation.

YOU: Excuse me, do you have any sunscreen I can use? (Opener #1)

HIM: Sure—here you go.

YOU: Thanks. By the way—do you know if there are any good surf schools around here? I've been meaning to learn to surf for a while. (Opener #2)

HIM: Yeah, totally—Joe's Surf School is awesome. I instruct there every now and again.

YOU: Is it difficult? I mean, how do you know where the waves are going to break? (Follow-up)

HIM: Oh, that part is easy. You just watch the waves from the beach. The hard part is learning to stand up!

Now you've met the guy that no one else could figure out how to meet.

To Sit or Not to Sit:
The Ups and Downs of Seating Logistics

Let's say that your target Hot Guy is sitting with his posse of Hot Friends at a table in your favorite bar. How do you deal with this? Most people think that you should remain standing until the conversation has become developed enough that you feel like it would be OK to sit down.

I don't agree. Here's why:

If you remain standing for a while and then sit down, the sitting down takes on a lot of significance. By waiting to sit down, you are communicating to the Hot Guys when you sit down that you dig them enough to sit with them. This throws your neutral status out the window. If you instead sit down as soon as possible, preferably right after the guy or guys have given you a response to your initial opener, you are able to maintain your neutrality. You will also come off as a totally confident and hip chick who feels that it is completely fine to sit with strangers and talk.

This may sound strange to you. It is not normally socially acceptable to bust into a group's conversation and then sit with them. However, in this case, you are asking a neutral question, listening to their response, liking it, and then sitting down to continue the discussion. It is not socially awkward because you are projecting that you don't think it is weird at all. In fact, what you project is that it is normal and cool to sit immediately. And because you don't think it is weird, they won't even stop to think about it. They will just assume it's normal.

Let's take a look at an example so you can see what I mean:

YOU [standing]: Guys. Can you explain something to me? Why is it that guys feel the need to hog the remote control? I was just watching TV with some of my guy friends before I came here tonight, and they would not let go of the remote, even during commercials. They kept telling me, "Girls aren't allowed to have the remote." What is that about?

HIM [sitting]: Ha-ha. Yeah, I guess guys do kind of hog the remote. I think it's some kind of power thing.

YOU [sitting down as you speak and leaning in to hear better]: Really? It seems like such a minor thing to have control of. What do they think the girl is going to do with the remote? Break it? What are they afraid of?

HIM: Well, blah blah blah.

Counterintuitive as it may seem, this is by far the best way to deal with a group of seated people. If you're a fairly confident girl, and there's not enough room, you could even say "Move over a bit, will you?" as you sit down. Instead of speaking to them as an outsider, you will move into the group and into the heart of the conversation by sitting down as soon as you can.

Sexy, Not Bitchy:
The Importance of Calibrated Teasing

I have stressed the importance of the neutral approach so that Hot Guy will have no clue you're hitting on him. But you have probably noticed that several of my example openers poke fun at the male population or guy behavior in general, right from the start: for instance, how guys hog the remote or how they grunt in the gym. Immediately thereafter, I suggest telling the guy he looks like a "hogger" or a "grunter." This is a feisty way of flirting, and it works fantastically for several reasons:

1. It's funny! How often can you can call someone a "grunter" in everyday conversation and get away with it? Plus, it's true. And both sexes will appreciate your keen eye for the hilarious subtleties of the average male. You are also coming across as fun and cool right from the start, and that is a very good thing.

2. It's much more comfortable for a guy to have a girl come up to him and tease him about his gender's neuroses than it is for her to gushingly tell him what beautiful eyes he has.

3. Joking around and being feisty, although a form of flirting, will put much less pressure on the whole

interaction. This is because you are not letting him know outright that you think he's cute. You're just teasing him a little bit.

Busting on your Hot Guy is essentially flirting behind the smoke screen that says "I'm teasing you because I'm not interested," when what you actually mean is "I think you're cute, so I'm going to tease you." This is a tried-and-true tactic in the dating world, having developed in the kindergarten sandbox. It is neutral because the person on the receiving end cannot with any certainty tell whether the teaser is teasing him because she likes him or because he looks like he would be fun to tease. He may have his suspicions about where you stand, but he won't know for sure. This keeps you firmly on neutral ground. It's a little cocky to do this, but it works like a charm.

Caveat: out of everything I talk about in this book, this is the one skill that takes practice, practice, practice if you're not used to doing it. If you don't tease enough, he's not going to notice. If you tease too much, he's going to think you're a bitch with a chip on your shoulder. My suggestion is to test out what you feel is an appropriate level of teasing for the situation and tweak the level up or down depending on how the Hot Guy reacts. Treat these experiments like the practice runs they are and don't take it personally if things don't go exactly as planned. Remember, there are plenty of Hot Guys out there for the taking.

You will pick up on what level of teasing is acceptable in what situation very quickly. For example, if you're in a bar, joking around is completely natural—even expected. In a coffee shop, anything more than very gently teasing the guy you just met would be a little much.

What to Do When the Hot Guy Is in a Group

What if your target is in a group of guys or, even more intense, in a group of both guys and other girls?

This is fairly advanced stuff. I highly recommend that you get comfortable opening just one guy on his own or two guys together before you start tackling large groups of guys or groups of guys and girls. Once you are satisfied that you rock with single guys and guys with one other male friend—welcome to the jungle.

GROUPS OF GUYS

One thing you will find when you start opening groups is that groups of guys behave very differently from groups of girls.

Surprising as it may seem, guys are not really that competitive with their friends over girls. If a girl comes into the group and one of the guys seems to really like her, the other guys will back down, even if they also like the girl. They do this out of respect for their friendship. Generally (and unfortunately), the more attractive guys will stand down because they figure they have plenty of opportunities with girls anyway. They seem to feel that it is unfair to monopolize the girl who has come into their group. These hotter guys will often even excuse themselves in order to leave the less attractive guy with a "shot" at the girl. This can be extremely frustrating if the only reason you came into the group in the first place was to meet the Hot Guy, and you got stuck with his somewhat less attractive friend: this has happened to me a LOT!

The solution to this is easy: guys are realistic. The Hot Guy will let the not-so-attractive friend have a shot at the hot girl, but if it is clear that she likes someone else (the Hot Guy), then it becomes OK in the guy code of honor for the Hot Guy to talk with her. The not-so-attractive guy will just figure that it wasn't his lucky night.

Just as with the lone Hot Guys, when approaching large groups of guys, come into the group neutral. Don't show interest in any of the guys—you are just a cool chick with a question you need answered.

Then, as the conversation gets going (and after about five minutes), it is fine to start showing an interest in one guy more than the others. Do not do this overtly, but definitely do it enough so that the other guys take the hint.

For example, maybe you make more eye contact with Hot Guy than you do with his friends. Maybe you laugh a little more at his jokes. And when they all start speaking at once, you turn and listen to what Hot Guy is saying, so it is his conversational thread that gets picked up. Then, perhaps you touch him lightly on the arm as you laugh at one of his jokes when you haven't touched any of the other guys.

Don't be mean to any one member of the group; just subtly let it be known that you have an interest in one of them (Hot Guy) over the others. Guys are pretty well attuned to these signals, and they will realize if you prefer one in the group. They will usually give in fairly easily at this point and bud off into another group, joking ruefully about how Jeff always gets the hot girls, or some such thing, leaving the two of you alone to get better acquainted.

GROUPS OF GUYS AND GIRLS

For a group with both guys and other girls, the rules are very similar to what you do with a group of just guys, with a few extra tips.

The very best way to deal with the other girls is just to chat to them as you would to the other guys in the group. Make plenty of eye contact with them, include them in the conversation, and, above all, always be friendly toward them. We can all, as women, smell a bitch from a mile away. If you are one of those girls whose friends are predominantly male, and a girl comes in and ignores you, you know what I'm talking about. It is extremely important for that girl in the group to like you. If her guy friends sense that she is picking up something negative from you, they will most likely lose interest as well. She is essentially one of the guys, and if she's respected in the group, they won't jeopardize their friendship for an outsider. On the flip side, if she likes you and warms to you, the guys will follow suit.

This isn't universal of course: there are girls who defend their territory ferociously, despite your best attempts to be cool toward them. If this happens, just play it the best you can and continue to be calm and neutral. The guys will probably have realized what she's like, and if you maintain a cool, friendly approach in the face of the unfriendly force, they will think better of you for it.

If the girl is the girlfriend of one of the guys there, or she *wants* to be the girlfriend of one of the guys there, she will soon let you know who is off-limits. If she thinks you seem like a cool person, she'll be happy for you to meet the other guys in the group. Since you came in with a neutral approach, she will assume like the guys that you are just a cool, sociable girl who had something on her mind and decided to confidently chat with some strangers about it. A neutral approach is very nonthreatening, and if your opener is fun, you may well make their evening with your entertaining observations.

To recap, when approaching large groups of guys or groups of guys and girls, the rules remain the same as when you are approaching a single Hot Guy or a Hot Guy with his friend: remain neutral. When talking to other girls in the group, remain friendly and cool.

The Unspoken Word: Body Language

No dating book would be complete without a discussion about body language, right? I won't to go into it very much: any socially calibrated woman is going to be able to tune her body language to the social situation at hand very skillfully. But I have listed a few things to watch out for here, just in case.

1. **Eye contact.** If you want to make a neutral approach on a guy, don't stare at him before you approach. This isn't neutral. The ideal situation is that he has checked you out but doesn't think you have seen him.

2. **Body Position.** When you first open Hot Guy, it is better not to turn fully toward him. This expresses interest and is therefore not neutral. Instead, turn only slightly toward him. This is congruent with someone who is thinking about something (for example, why guys hog the remote control and never let girls touch it) and decides to turn toward the nearest guy to ask him why guys do that. As the conversation gets going and gets more personal, turning in to face the guy is natural: you've liked what he said, and you're now expressing interest in him. He'll notice and will think it was all him that caused you to be interested, which will make him happy.

3. **Touch.** Once you've gotten to the point in the conversation where you're showing a bit more interest (i.e., in the Building Rapport phase), and he's enthusiastic about the conversation, it can be very helpful to let him know that you are now officially interested. Because you approached neutrally, he won't be sure whether you're just a friendly girl or you actually think he's a Hot Guy. Give him a break and let him know by inserting some touching into the conversation.

For example, when he says something funny, lean forward and touch his arm as you laugh. Don't leave your hand there (that can be creepy)—a two- or three-second touch is perfect. If you're sitting down, another good place is his thigh directly above his knee, which is a sexier place (just don't squeeze—a lot of people are really ticklish there). If the thigh feels too sexy or bold for you, his shoulder is a good bet (it's more in the "friend" zone but is a good place to start if you're nervous).

There are no hard-and-fast ground rules about when exactly to begin the touching, because every conversation will be different. Basically, if you can sense he's into it, go ahead and touch. If you can sense he's not, focus on building more rapport and drawing him out a bit with questions and stories of your own. If you're not sure of his interest, try the shoulder. If he's weirded out by your move, 99 percent of the time, he'll express that with his facial expression while the touching is happening—just look at his face while you touch his shoulder and you'll be able to tell what he thinks. If he likes it, he might smile or even blush—in which case you can move on to the arm or leg. If he doesn't like it, you'll know.

One note to remember about touching—some people don't like to be touched until they are much more comfortable with you. If he acts really strangely when you try the shoulder or arm touch, back off and let him touch you first. It should be enough to express your interest. Also, I recommend not doing the leg touch unless you're pretty sure of his interest. It's an overt move and leaves little room for maneuvering if he reacts badly.

Conversation Pieces: Using Your Wardrobe as an In

Again, no dating book would be complete without this part (and, again, any socially adjusted female will have this down and then some). I only have one thing I'd like to mention here:

If you have something that is unusual (i.e., a conversation piece), wear it.

If a guy has a legitimate reason to open you, he probably will. Wearing an unusual sweater, shirt, pants, bracelet, necklace, or hat gives guys an easy route into conversation with you, even if it is a slightly obvious route.

I wear this necklace that I found at a thrift store all the time, and it averages about five comments per night. Not all of the guys who open me by talking about my necklace are guys that I would necessarily want to talk to, but it's always a good confidence booster to have guys approaching me.

Plus, with an interesting piece, the guy you approach may well use it to start a conversational thread.

How to Use These Techniques in Online Dating

I encourage going out and approaching guys in person because you have so many more cues to use to determine if you like him and if he likes you back. Body language, tone of voice, smell, and where you met all tell you volumes about who he is and how the interaction is going. With on-line dating, you only have words to go by.

An important thing to remember about online dating is that it is a numbers game, just like regular pickup. You're not going to like every guy you go out with, and chances are good that you'll have to go out with more guys from the Internet than you would if you had met them in person. This is because, again, you have less information to go on from the start, so more has to be gathered on the actual date. If you met them for the first time in person (as you do in regular pickup), this wouldn't be an issue.

That being said, there are times when online dating can be great, such as when you're too tired to go out.

Another excellent side effect of being female and using online dating is a massive ego boost. If you're post-breakup and you need to ease into the dating scene again, make an online profile. You'll have twenty-five new messages twenty-four hours later from guys begging you to respond. They won't all be cute, and most of them won't be compatible with you, but who doesn't like a little appreciation?

I won't go into profile development and picture selection here, because I'm assuming you, as a sassy girl, already have

Screw Cupid: The Sassy Girl's Guide to Picking Up Hot Guys

a handle on that aspect. However, the biggest issue I hear about online dating is getting your chosen Hot Guy to respond to your emails.

The solution to that problem is below.

The ideas behind approaching a Hot Guy in person and approaching him online are the same.

1. You want to remain neutral to remove any sexual subtext from the approach.
2. You have to gain proximity neutrally. In other words, you need to have some other reason to be talking to him besides him.
3. You need to have some follow-up conversation prepared. The bonus about online dating is that you have time to think about what you could follow up while you're waiting for him to reply. It depends on the online site, but for most of them you have the option of directly instant messaging or emailing the Hot Guy.

For example, when I found a Hot Guy's profile I liked, I scanned it for anything that I was remotely interested in knowing more about. He had several mentions of doing triathlons, which was something I had been mildly interested in trying. I emailed him the following:

Hi CR175TriMan! I saw on your profile that you do triathlons. I've been interested in getting into that scene for a while but have no idea where to begin. Do you think you could tell me more about it? Any tips you have would be really helpful. Thanks!

He replied the next day, offering to meet me for coffee to answer any questions I might have. The date happened, and triathlons were discussed in detail for the first twenty minutes or so. After that, we started exchanging personal information such as what we did for a living, likes and interests, and where we lived. It ended up being a great date.

I found out later from him that he wasn't sure if I was just interested in the triathlons or in him. Because of the ambiguity, he was more interested than he would have normally been. He had a hot profile picture and said he got ten to fifteen new emails a week from girls asking him out. He chose to go out with me because he was intrigued.

The added bonus of having a conversation topic already planned out before the date was that there wasn't any awkward silence. Triathlons are an extensive subject, and I could have happily kept on chatting about them for an hour or more. As it turns out, we clicked fairly quickly, so that wasn't necessary.

Many of my friends scan Craigslist "Missed Connections" on a daily basis, searching for someone who may have "missed" them, and posting their missed connections with Hot Guys they've encountered. This can be great if you actually end up finding your missed connection and meeting them for a date, as you know you've already got something in common: a romantic streak. However, I'd like to say here that if you use the techniques in this book, you won't have "missed connections" anymore.

Before you learned how to pick up any guy, anytime, anywhere, it may have been your reality to hope that the Hot Guy you saw in the grocery store this morning thought you were equally Hot and will go home and post his missed connection with you. Now, you don't need to do that. You can meet him right then, right there and set up a date. Cool, huh? So, while I think Craigslist Missed Connections are fun to read and are perhaps good for killing some time on your lunch break, they're not a necessary part of your dating life.

The bottom line for online dating is to be ambiguous about your interest in the Hot Guy. About 99 percent of the time, he'll email you back just to find out if it was the other thing you're interested in or him. From there, you can suggest meeting for coffee or a drink to talk about the other thing, and hopefully sparks will fly.

The Brief and Mandatory Note on Safety

It makes me sad that I feel the need to mention this. It would be fantastic if everyone was nice to each other and there was no violence or anger in the world, but unfortunately there is.

I know you know how to keep yourself safe, and you know that I have to say something about it, so here it is:

Trust your instincts.

If the guy seems off, or you pick up on something that says you may be in danger, leave the situation as quickly and as safely as you can. Don't approach men who are alone when there is no one else around. Don't meet a guy for the first time in a private place; meet him in a public restaurant or a bar or somewhere equally busy. Do not go home with anyone without letting someone know where you will be. Always take your cell phone and pepper spray with you when you go out. And always, ALWAYS wear a condom. Safety comes first—no matter how cute he is.

Crap Advice: The right guy will always come to you. Trust destiny that one day he'll knock on your door and sweep you off your feet.

Why Is It crap? It's the "one day" of that statement that bites. "One day" could be next week, but it could also be two weeks after your ninety-fifth birthday. Why not take control of your dating happiness? You get out what you put in—put in some effort, and you'll have fifty Mr. Rights to choose from. Put in no effort, and you may find yourself involuntarily spending your Friday and Saturday nights in the company of your cat, eating ice cream, and watching Knight-in-Shining-Armor-Sweeps-Girl-Off-Her-Feet chick flicks.

3

you

I Have Choices—Now What?

So, now that the "How do I meet him?" part is settled, the next logical question is this: Now that I've got the skills to meet any guy, anywhere, anytime—what is it that I want in a guy?

This is something I battled with when I began to have choices. I thought I wanted one thing, but the more I looked for and dated that one thing, the more it became abundantly apparent that this one thing was not going to work for me.

The majority of the advice I read while figuring out how to pick up guys would say to make the most of the guys who come across your path. It isn't, according to them, about what you want. It's about making the most of what you've got. This is totally untrue.

From now on, if a dude does something that bugs you, lose his number. If he flakes on you, drop him. If he has an annoying trait that you know you will never get over, lose him. You don't ever have to put up with something that bothers you because you think that is the best you can do at the moment. You can meet any guy, anytime, anywhere. It is just a matter of finding the ones who work for you.

This is quite a paradigm shift from how we think about guys. Many will advise girls to not rule anybody out, to give people time to grow on them. But as I pointed out earlier, this is a viewpoint based on scarcity. If you think you're only going to be meeting two guys this month, it makes sense to give your number to the guy who has a penchant for shooting rabbits on the weekend. Maybe you could get over that, in time. But if you're meeting ten guys a week, Bunny Killer isn't going to even register as a blip on your Hot Guy radar.

What Is the "Click Factor"?

The truth is, each woman on this earth is probably only completely and from-the-start comfortably compatible with a handful of guys.

Do you know that awesome feeling you get with someone when you "click" with him? And not just on one level—have you ever met that person you hang with for twenty minutes and then discover you're finishing each other's sentences? This is the click where you feel like you can spill your secrets and this person will completely understand you. Some people call this other person your soul mate; I call it the Click Factor.

For the average person, this feeling occurs with maybe ten

people over the course of a lifetime. If I think back, I would estimate that I've met about a thousand guys in my life, and I've really clicked with six of them so far. Six!! Even if we assume that I've clicked with ten, my ratio is still only 1 in 100. So, as compatibility goes, the odds of clicking with the average random guy are 1 percent.

That said, why waste your time talking for one second longer than you need to with someone you are not compatible with? There are so many more people to meet who may end up being one of the ones you click with.

In order to find those guys that you click with, two things need to happen. First, you need to identify your List—your needs in a mate. The List consists of traits that you desire in a mate, compiled by knowing what you know about yourself and whom you get along with. Second, you need to screen the guys you meet for your List traits as soon as possible after meeting them. It is a waste of your time to talk to the guys who do not have the click, because that time could be spent talking to the next guy who might.

The Importance of Figuring Out Your List of "Hell No"s and "Must Have"s

Every girl on earth has a list of things that she screens potential boyfriends for. It is a personal list, compiled over years of meeting losers who added to the "cannot stand this" column and meeting awesome people who added to the "must have this" column.

For some of us, this list is very long. For others, it is very short. Here is mine, as an example:

- Must not be religious. (I'm spiritual but not into organized religion. I've found out that, despite dating several intensely religious guys, it just does not work with my belief system. I respect guys' beliefs but can't live with them.)
- A dry wit and a wicked sense of humor is a very good thing.
- An open, accepting, and exploratory mind is a very, very good thing.
- Must not take life too seriously. I am here to have fun and enjoy the moment—not live five years from now.
- Intelligent. I dig a guy who can teach me something I don't know yet.
- Confidence is huge. Insecurities should be kept to a minimum.
- Huge and exploratory sex drive—to match mine.
- Ambitious. I've got wild dreams. I want someone to dream wild with and do wild with.
- Adventurous and active. I love to exercise, and I love adventuring.

Your List may be longer. It may be shorter. What's important is that this list reflects who you are and who you want to be with, because this ideal person will be the person who fills the boyfriend role. It is extremely important for compatibility's sake that the List truly reflect who you are as a person and not what you think you want in a boyfriend.

For a bit of humor, go to this site: www.spam.abuse. net/picky_calc.html. You will find that no matter what you enter, the answer is always zero. Let this serve as an entertaining reminder that too much List equals lonely nights with *Sex and the City* and a carton of Häagen-Dazs.

There is a question you can ask yourself about each item on your List, just to make sure that your List really reflects your current self. If there are any latent items on your List that are there not from self-discovery but are from other sources (i.e., the media, your friends, your mother), it is important to make sure that these things really belong. If your List isn't accurate, the risk is that you may inadvertently screen away a guy who may have had the click.

The best way to make sure your List is accurate and true to you and you alone is to look at each individual item and ask yourself the question, "What about that is important to me?"

To demonstrate what I mean, I'll talk about a girl I once knew named Eva. Eva constantly talked about wanting to date a guy with a PhD. She would scope out the nearby university as often as possible and would only date guys who passed her "Do you have a PhD?" test—and no one else. It turns out Eva grew up in a family and community where PhDs were unheard of, which she hated. She felt that if she dated guys who had PhDs, she could get away from her background and live a more enlightened life than the one she saw growing up.

If Eva were to ask herself the "What about that is important to me?" question with her PhD requirement, the internal conversation would go something like this:

"I want a guy with a PhD."

What about that is important to me?

"I don't want to live the same life my mother did, because I didn't like what I saw of her life."

What about that is important to me?

"I'm embarrassed I didn't come from a background of

higher education, and I'm worried that if I don't 'date up,' I'm going to end up just like her."

Eva has realized that the real reason behind her PhD absolute is that she's embarrassed about where she came from. Now she can ask herself the question, "Is dating a dude with a PhD the only way I can get over feeling embarrassed about my roots?"

The answer is clearly no. There are tons of other ways she could get over that feeling: she could take a look at her own perceptions of her self-worth and figure out why she thinks it's such a bad thing to have come from where she came from; she could take matters into her own hands and try for that job or master's degree or even PhD herself. Either way, in this case, the root of her feeling had nothing to do with the guy she dated and everything to do with her internal perceptions. Even if she had married a guy with a PhD, it probably wouldn't have gotten her over her embarrassment of her roots.

Just for example's sake, let's assume Eva wanted a guy with a PhD for a totally different reason:

"I want a guy with a PhD."

What about that is important to me?

"I want to date a guy who is smart."

What about that is important to me?

"I want great conversation with a guy who is intelligent."

Then she asks herself, "Are guys with PhDs the only intelligent guys who are capable of great conversation?" Again, no. There are many, many guys who are capable of intelligent, witty conversation who don't have the elusive PhD.

The Eva in both situations got hung up on a certain trait (guy having PhD) and screened out hundreds of potentials because they didn't have those three letters after their names. If Eva had examined the reasons behind her mandatory PhD requirement, she could have had a lot more dates, or perhaps she would have met her click guy by now.

Don't sell yourself short by screening out "good ones" because you haven't examined the true reasons behind a List trait. Even if you're sure your List is spot on, it may be worth your while to double-check, just to make sure.

How to Screen for the Click

Screening is probably not a new concept for you. It happens every time you talk to a new guy. However, what you may or may not know is that screening for the click can happen as early as the opening line.

My definition of screening is checking to see if the potential Hot Guy you're talking to has the nonnegotiable traits on your List.

I recommend doing as much screening as you can *in the first thirty minutes.*

If you're Jewish and you absolutely cannot fathom dating outside your faith, find out ASAP if the guy you're talking to fits the bill. If he doesn't, move on. There is no point in spending any more time than you have to talking to the non-Jewish guy if there's no way it will work. (Of course, if you're just out to meet new people, knock yourself out.) It is much better to find out that Hot Guy isn't Jewish after ten minutes than two hours into Date #1.

So what's the best way to do this?

Directly interrogating Hot Guy at the bar won't get you very far. Not only is interrogation usually considered a socially awkward form of communication, but he'll feel like he's being probed. If he senses that he is being potentially eliminated by saying the wrong thing, he is going to be on guard and act defensive (who wouldn't?). After all, he doesn't know what your dealbreaker is, and guys are just as insecure about rejection as we are.

The best way to screen is to have planned topics of conversation that are innocent on the surface but also give you clues as to whether he's a potential click.

For example, let's say that you are screening for a guy who knows what's what financially and has a decent portfolio: you are sick of dating the freeloaders who don't know how to balance their checkbooks. You could get a pretty good indication of Hot Guy's situation with the following conversation:

YOU: Isn't it interesting how well the new iPhone is selling? It seems like everyone is buying one.

HIM: Yeah. A lot of my friends have them—I'm thinking of getting one, too.

YOU: It seems like all this new technology is bringing up the prices of quite a few tech stocks. You would think people would have been burned by the housing crisis. I know my stocks took quite a hit.

(Answer #1) HIM: Yeah, mine, too—I don't think I'll be going into the market again for a while.

(Or Answer #2) HIM: Are you kidding? The housing crisis was wicked. My dad made a ton of money with his mortgage company and totally bought me this foosball table—I got to quit my job and play it all day long! Yeah!

If your List has traits that you cannot bend on, you have your reasons, and coming up with subtle screens for those traits should be a piece of cake. However, I want to throw out there that having prepared topics that automatically do the screening will make your life a lot easier. You won't have to think on the fly, and you can use them every single time you screen: the guys will never know you are recycling.

Also, once you start meeting a lot of guys every night, working these screens into the first thirty minutes of conversation is a huge time- and trouble-saver for you. Coming home after a three-hour conversation with Hot Guy and realizing you forgot to check how tall he was is not an ideal situation if shorter guys are a big no-no for you.

Know what your deal breakers are and screen for them as soon as you can.

Quiz:
True or False:

You get into a conversation with a Hot Guy and find out you have some political differences, at which point he bails (politely) on the conversation and leaves. This makes him an asshole.

Answer: False.

Guys have things they look for in relationships, just like we do. The Hot Guy in this situation clearly had an issue with girls having different political leanings from his own. If anything, it was a good thing he bailed—at least he won't waste any more of your time when he knows it will never work.

⌣

him
(the hot guy)

You've Got to Do More
than Just Show Up

Iɴ my vast research to see if anyone else had an easy answer to the questions I was asking about picking up guys (which they didn't), I found loads and loads of feel-good fantasy fodder:

"You're wonderful and special and any guy would be happy to date you!" If that is true, then why did Ryan Masters destroy my ego?

"Think happy thoughts and you'll be the most attractive girl in the room." I was thinking happy thoughts when I asked to buy all of those guys drinks, and it clearly did not have the effect of making me the most attractive girl in the room. If it did, I would not have felt like slime mold.

I also saw some advice: "So he's not into you? Here's a trick to change his mind!" This certainly makes us all feel better. Who doesn't like hearing that you're the most wonderful, special person *ever* and if by any chance the guy you've chosen hasn't noticed this, there is a simple trick you can do that will change his mind *and* make him fall totally and completely head over heels in love with you?

Reality check: this advice rarely (if ever) works; unfortunately, we don't always land the guy we want. Sometimes he appears to be more interested in someone else or he's just not interested in you, period. He's not a jerk; all men aren't assholes—he just doesn't have it for you.

The truth, however harsh and scary and unwelcome it may be, is that guys have things they are looking for, too. If you don't have what they want, they will move on (or not notice you to begin with).

Sometimes it is a question of compatibility. You are Susie Democrat, and he is a Billy the Hard-core Republican, so it wouldn't have worked out anyway.

But sometimes, as far as you're concerned, everything was beautiful. You were starting to allow yourself to dream wedding bells, and then all of a sudden he up and decides he's not into you anymore—three weeks into the relationship! So what happened?

The answer may have been you just didn't have something that he wanted. Guys are no different from women in that respect. If he finds something that qualifies as a deal breaker, you're not going to be the one for him no matter how perfect everything felt on your side.

This brings me to my final piece in the formula: for success with the male population, these three things need to happen.

1. **Get your numbers up.** You've got to meet enough guys to meet the guys who have the click.

2. **Know your List.** Otherwise, you're likely to keep ending up with something (or someone) you don't want.

3. **You've got to bring enough to the table.** Guys have Lists, too.

It's not enough to just show up. There is a perception in society that women just have to look hot in a relationship. Despite the shallow stereotype, men have emotional needs as well, and a healthy, mature relationship involves reciprocity. Both parties have needs, and if one party's needs are not being met, that party will go elsewhere to satisfy them. It's as simple as that. Sounds fair, no?

So while your ideal guy may be picked out and you go and have that fantastic conversation with him, he is also figuring out whether you are or are not what he is looking for. Therefore, rather than ignoring this frequently avoided fact, look at how to maximize your chances of being the Ms. Right for your Mr. Right.

What Do Guys Find Attractive?

I convinced my friend Leah to use my methods for meeting guys one night when we were out bar-hopping. I gave her the basics, and she acted as my female wing. We opened maybe five groups of guys with no problems at all. All of them warmed to us immediately, and the conversations were fun and unstrained. Leah had a blast and loved that it was so easy. Not one of the guys acted like a jerk, and none of them had any clue they were being hit on.

Afterward, I asked her what she thought of my approaches. She replied, "This is awesome. I had no idea there were cool guys out there—I thought they were all jerks! But it doesn't matter. I'm not hot enough."

My response to her was in three parts.

1. **When it is neutral, sexual attraction is irrelevant.**
2. **Guys differ widely in what they find attractive.**
3. **There are things you can do to become more attractive.**

Here is a breakdown on each.

When the Interaction Is Neutral, Attraction is Irrelevant

First off, Leah misunderstood the dynamic you get with a neutral opener.

These guys don't know that they are being hit on. They don't even *suspect* that they're being hit on. They think a fun, sociable, confident (Hot) girl has happened to fall into conversation with them (lucky them!). Almost any guy is happy to spend a few minutes talking to almost anyone (male or female) if that person seems friendly, normal, and fun.

For example, I've had fun conversations with eighty-year-old men at bus stops. Does this mean that I thought the nice old man was hot and I was desperate to get into his pants? Of course not. Humans are social by nature, and if we can enjoy a fun, random conversation with someone fun and new, we will.

Neutrally opening someone is just a way of getting into that random conversation without setting off the guy's alarm bells that he is your sexual target. The conversation is followed by a fun chat, during the course of which his attraction to you and your attraction to him may or may not develop. Leah's misunderstanding probably came from every female's experience of getting hit on by guys.

When a guy comes up to a girl in a bar and says, "Can I buy you a drink?" or "Hi! I'm Brent," it pressures her to make a decision about him then and there. If she doesn't find him attractive enough, he's not her type, or whatever reason he's bugging her, he runs a 99 percent chance of being shot down immediately.

Why?

Because what she really heard when he said "Hi" was "Hi—I want to have sex with you. Do you want to have sex with me?" If she doesn't find him extremely attractive, her immediate response is, "Hell no, I don't even want to meet you."

In addition, by making it extraordinarily obvious that he is interested, he has suddenly made the interaction a sexual one. If she doesn't find him sexually attractive, the guy has more of a chance of sprouting billy goat horns and a prehensile tail than getting the girl's number.

However, by opening someone neutrally and letting it flow into natural conversation, the interaction is not sexual in the slightest. If you are just asking him a question, he has no reason to judge you in a sexual manner. Sure, sexual attraction may develop as you talk more, but at the beginning sex is not a factor. He is simply a vehicle for the answer to your question.

If, after your opener, your target guy looks awkward and he didn't seem like the shy type, chances are you didn't do the opener well. Maybe your body language or your tone told him that you were sexually interested and so he decided that you were probably trying to pick him up. The key is to turn off the sexual component of your interaction. If this is done completely, you will come across as just a fun, chatty, sociable girl who happens to have said something to him simply because you needed some information and you thought he could help.

So, regardless of how hot you think you are or are not, there's absolutely nothing stopping you from having a ton of great interactions every time you go out.

Porn as Proof: Guys Are All Over the Map in What They Find Attractive

Even if my lovely friend Leah accepts that it's OK for her to open guys because it is not about sex when you open someone neutrally, that's not really all she was saying. What she was really saying is, "Even if it were easy for me to get to meet lots of great guys, I'm nothing like the societal standard of beauty, and all guys want that. Therefore, no one will be sexually interested in me."

Leah is making a huge mistake in her reasoning.

"I'm nothing like the societal standard of beauty." True. Leah is very good-looking, but it's unlikely she's going to end up as the cover model for a fashion magazine.

"All guys want a beautiful woman." Well, *beautiful* is one of those words that seems to define something specific. Actually, its meaning can be on opposite ends of the spectrum, depending on who is doing the talking. The statement "All straight guys want a girl they're attracted to" is much more accurate. Leah is making the assumption that all guys want what society, in general, decides is beautiful, but she is totally and completely incorrect.

For a start, have a look around next time you go out. There are guys with women of all shapes, sizes, and levels of hotness. I think it's fair to say that these guys must be attracted to the women they're with; otherwise, they wouldn't be with them.

"But those guys aren't cute."

"But maybe the guys are just settling."

"But maybe they're just lonely."

Stop for a second. There are probably some relationships in your immediate circle that may not make sense to you but in which you can tell that both parties are very much into each other. I can think of twelve relationships off the top of my head in which a great guy is in a great relationship with a girl who doesn't look like she just walked off a magazine cover. And yet he is very into her, he is sexually attracted to her, and they have a fantastic relationship. How is this possible if all guys are attracted only to physical perfection?

Furthermore, pornography would not exist without guys to fuel the fire, and there are successful websites for huge boobs, small boobs, skinny girls, 300-pound girls, and everything in between. I feel the media-reinforced view that women need to look like supermodels at all times is completely ridiculous. There is porn out there for every taste and every fetish you can imagine, and there are *countless* porn sites that have absolutely nothing to do with traditional standards of beauty. Why would guys be choosing to look at this stuff if it didn't turn them on? Why would they be paying money to download movies of "normal-looking" girls if they did not want to watch them?

The truth of the matter is that guys have a *very* wide range of sexual tastes. Sexuality is a wonderfully diverse thing.

Take three guys at random: one could be into S&M with a leather fetish, one could have a foot fetish and get off on looking at girls on red balloons, and another might only get turned on when he sees girls in white T-shirts. You just don't know. And as far as psychologists can discover, and this author's vast research into the fetishes of the male population has revealed, there isn't any particular pattern to how sexual tastes are distributed and determined. There's just no way of knowing for sure what the Hot Guy is into before you get to know him (and check out his hard drive).

It is true that there are certain "norms" on which a lot of guys will agree. There are certain looks that are likely to attract more of a following than other looks will. But to say that no one will be sexually interested in you is totally and completely wrong—no matter what you look like.

Once you have accepted that there are guys out there who will find you attractive, it basically comes down to meeting enough guys to find them. As always, it is a numbers game, just like it is a numbers game for every woman on this planet. Even the famous ultra-beautiful actresses cannot expect that every guy they meet is going to fall head-over-heels in love with them.

Man Interview:
THERE ARE THINGS YOU CAN DO
TO BECOME MORE ATTRACTIVE

As I've already said, sexuality is a varied and wonderful thing. It is tempting to try and simplify or generalize it by saying things like, "Guys only like girls with small feet." But if that is true, why are there porn sites out there solely devoted to girls with huge feet?

In the opposite camp, I have heard guys saying that "Girls are just looking for a guy with money." But then why did I attend a wedding last summer where neither the bride nor the groom had enough money to go on a honeymoon and the main course at dinner was takeout Chinese food?

It makes the world seem more simple and more manageable if we can make generalizations apply to real life, but this is done at the expense of accuracy. Whoever you are, whatever you look like, there is a guy out there who will find you attractive. Period.

That said, I took it upon myself to informally interview as many guys as I could to try to get an accurate (albeit general) picture of what guys today find attractive. I interviewed them about what they found hot physically in a girl as well as what drove them wild about a girl's personality.

I'd like to state at this point that the answers I got from surveying these guys were not a function of how cute these guys were or how desperate they were. I personally thought that all the guys I talked to were cute, socially well adjusted, and fun. And I told them I was doing research for a book before I started getting their answers (which, by the way, is a great way to start a conversation), to undermine the possibility that they thought I was hitting on them and skewed their answers. On average, these guys were about thirty-five and had extremely varied professions (producer, lawyer, investment banker, consultant, mechanic, yoga instructor, etc.).

Their answers varied so much that it was impossible to list everything that everyone said. I've summarized below my best attempt at generalizing what they all said:

The Physical

If you can think of it, guys are into it. This one had a lot of different answers, so I'll do my best to boil it down: with the exception of a few guys who were into larger women or underweight women, it seems that, in general, guys are more attracted to a girl who is in shape and healthy than one who isn't.

Personality

Intelligence level must match theirs. There were a few exceptions, but it seems that guys tend to be attracted to a woman who is about as smart as they are. If she's too smart, they feel inferior. If they feel like they're smarter than the woman, they said it was harder to forge a connection.

A big heart. Warm-hearted and generous came up quite a few times in the good category. Stingy, selfish, and mean came up on the negative side.

Humorous. It appears the ability to make a guy laugh is highly valued.

Confident. Guys tend to prefer a woman who is confident over one who is not.

Similar philosophy and similar activities. It seems that guys like the girls who are into the same things they are more than they like girls who were into totally different things. However, there were a few exceptions who said that they'd like it if the girl was into something totally different but that they (the guy) hadn't tried yet.

No Baggage. The phrase "She's got to have her shit together" came up time and time again. It appears that baggage isn't a desired trait.

After this interesting foray into what the male (in general) prefers in the female he's dating (in general), I asked myself which seemed to be more important, the physical or personality?

The answer? It varied completely from guy to guy. If I had to wager a guess, I'd say that for about 70 percent of the guys I talked to, ideal personality traits were identified before ideal physical traits, and 90 percent of them listed both personality and physical traits.

So, given all this, what can be done to improve the chances of being found attractive by the guys you find attractive?

In the physical camp, being fit and healthy is not only better for you in life, but it appears guys in general find fit and healthy more attractive. Since this is not a book about working out and eating right, I won't go into this. There are many much more qualified professionals out there with hundreds of great magazines, websites, books, TV shows, and the like that deal explicitly with getting into shape and living a healthy lifestyle.

In the personality camp, each one of us is different and unique, and that's what makes us fabulous. Period.

However, one of the great things about being human is that without losing that part of ourselves that we feel is intrinsically us, it is very possible to choose the ideas and experiences that have beneficial impacts on us. We can choose who we want to become, and we can seek out the ideas and experiences that will help us get there.

For evolutionary reasons, there is a very strong correlation between what men find attractive in women and which personality traits in women lead them to have strong, happy, centered, successful lives. This is because a man is biologically programmed to seek out a mate who will give him the children with the best chance of survival. The better adapted and successful at life a woman is, the greater the chance her children will be well adapted and successful at life, too (in both genetic and developmental ways). The same, of course, applies in reverse: a woman looks for a man who is a survivor.

What this means is that your best bet for becoming more attractive (in general) is simply to go out and try to make your life as great as you can.

Learn new things, expose yourself to new ideas, and seek out new experiences. Get to know yourself as well as you can, and explore those recesses of dreams and desires that can lie buried deep inside. Bring as much happiness and wonder as you can into your life.

Quiz:
True or False:

There's a Hot Guy who has been checking you out. If he wants to talk to you, he'll come over. If he doesn't, he won't.

Answer: False.

Every time I go out with my best guy friends, one of the first things they do is scan the bar looking for girls they think are cute. Once they locate said cute girls, they spend the rest of the night salivating over them but never actually approaching them. This is because they chicken out. They are awesome guys—I would vouch for them in a second—but they've been burned one too many times to have the confidence to talk to every cute girl they come across. So, yes, while it is *possible* that the reason he's not approaching is because he doesn't want to talk to you, the much more likely explanation is that he's too scared.

the
full package

Hᴇʀᴇ ɪꜱ ᴀ whole entire interaction so that you can see how it all fits together.

You're sitting at a table in a bar with your friends. Hot Guy is with his friend at the bar, chatting and occasionally watching the TV. Without looking at Hot Guy, you approach the bar and happen to stand close to him as you wait for the bartender to get round to you. After a brief pause, you open Hot Guy and his friend in a friendly but slightly exasperated way:

> ʏᴏᴜ: Hey, guys—can you explain something to me? I was in the gym today, and there was this guy in there grunting while he was working out. You could hear him all the way across the room! Why do guys feel the need to do that? Women don't grunt, so it must be biologically possible for guys not to, no?

> ʜᴏᴛ ɢᴜʏ: Heh-heh. Yeah, a lot of guys do grunt in the gym.

FRIEND: (laughing) Totally. Guys grunt all the time.

YOU: (with trepidation) You guys don't grunt, do you?

HOT GUY: (smiling) No, I don't grunt . . . OK, maybe I do occasionally if I'm doing a really tough set.

FRIEND: I totally grunt. It's the only manly option. (He turns to Hot Guy.) Hey, man, Julie just walked in. I'll catch you later. (He smiles at you and leaves.)

YOU: I knew it! You're both grunters! Oh my god, I can't believe I'm talking to grunters!

HOT GUY: (laughing) Hey, I don't grunt *that* much. And women totally grunt, too. Look at tennis—a lot of the girls make grunt noises. Sometimes it's more of a squeak than a grunt, but it can still be pretty loud.

YOU: Well, that is true . . . but this guy was really loud. It was like a 'YYYAAAAHHH' sound. What kind of sound do you make?

HOT GUY: I guess I make a kind of 'nnnnggggg' sound. It's very muted.

YOU: Hmmm. I'm not sure about that. I think I should steer clear of you. Which gym do you go to?

HOT GUY: I go to the Gold's Gym up on Fourteenth Street. How about you?

YOU: I go to the 24 Hour Fitness on Sixth. They have a lot of treadmills, which is good. I mainly go there to do cardio.

HOT GUY: Speaking of which, isn't it funny when you

get off the treadmill and you walk really weirdly? I've never really gotten used to that.

YOU: Yeah, I usually just stand around a bit after I get off so I don't look too much like a moron!

HOT GUY: Are you training for anything in particular or just for general fitness?

YOU: Well, I did a couple of triathlons earlier this year, and although I'm way too busy to keep up that level of training, I still want to at least maintain some kind of level of fitness.

HOT GUY: Oh? What else is keeping you so busy?

Let's pause here so that I can break down each section and insert some handy helpful commentary.

So—you come in with a neutral opener. You give no indication of being interested in the guy before you approach or while you get proximity. Your tone, body language, and what you say are all consistent with someone who has just had a memory of being in the gym earlier that day pop into her head, and being of a sociable disposition, decides to see if the guys next to her at the bar can shed any light on why guys grunt in the gym.

Hot Guy and his friend are amused by the fact that someone is puzzled by guy behavior, and they feel like this could be an amusing conversation to have, so they respond.

The Friend sees someone he wants to talk to enter the bar, so he takes off, leaving you with Hot Guy. His friend may have noticed that Hot Guy was vibing with you, or maybe he really did want to talk to Julie. Either way, the situation is now one-on-one, which is good.

Then you tease Hot Guy (gently), which gives the conversation a light, fun tone and also helps negate any suspicion that you might be hitting on him. It seems like your intention by commenting on the grunting is just to make fun of guys in general.

He enjoys the teasing and defends himself well by poking a little fun at women, but also in a nicely calibrated way.

You also get points for pitching your self-deprecation (by calling yourself a moron) at the proper level to be humorous, but not to the point where he starts to doubt your social skills. If you had belabored the point that you looked like a moron when you got off the treadmill any more than you did, he would start to develop a very clear mental image of you as a moron. He would also start to doubt your confidence in yourself, which doesn't breed sexiness. In this situation, though, you've done a great job of being funny by poking a little fun at yourself, without taking it so far as to appear that you have low self-esteem. This is good.

By now, about thirty seconds into the conversation, you can both sense that on the basis of the initial interaction, you might get along well. Neither of you has said anything that made the other one feel awkward or implied neediness. Both of you seem to be normal, functioning adults, and you've each made the other laugh. You have established that you both go to the gym. At this point, it is natural for you to move into getting-to-know-you conversation and finding commonalities.

Notice also that the guy's apparently innocent question "Are you training for anything in particular or just for general fitness?" may actually be a screen. One of his criteria for women he dates may be that he wants someone he can go running with or who might be a good tennis player (he already brought up tennis). When you bring up triathlons, you may have scored a hit, because that means you're active.

Let's continue:

YOU: Well, I just started a new business, actually. I'm developing a fashion line of women's dresses. It's a lot of work, but it's always been a dream of mine. I had a little money saved, and I figured I should go for it.

HOT GUY: (smiling) That's awesome!! I totally think you should go after the things you really want. How far along are you?

YOU: Well, I've got all the designs done, and I've started making some samples. There's a long way to go, but so far, so good. How about you? What do you do?

HOT GUY: I work for a marketing consulting firm. We advise clients about promotions and public relations.

YOU: Oh, really? Do you like it?

HOT GUY: Yeah, it's awesome. I get to think strategically about the best way to get someone's message out into the world. It's especially cool if the client has a product that I really feel is beneficial.

Although you did it very subtly, you set up a screen to see if he was just a cute guy at a bar or if he had a little more to him, like some ambition and passion. First, you mentioned that you were busy. The guy would not realize it, but this is inviting the question that he asked, namely, "What is keeping you so busy?"

This gives you the chance to talk about what you are doing. This then makes it much more natural for you to turn the question back on him and ask him what he does. Men don't like to be probed any more than women do, but if you have already volunteered information about yourself, guys will happily reciprocate.

Your question, "Do you like it?" (in reference to his job) is a great screening question. It is a concern for you that the guy be happy doing what he does for a living. It also gives an insight into what kind of guy he is—what drives and motivates him.

Back to the conversation:

YOU: Hey—are you any good at pool?

HOT GUY: Yeah—I've been known to do acceptably. Why, do you want a game?

YOU: Sure! Let's do it. But only if you think you're good enough to handle a master.

(Go play pool.)

This is also a screen.

How, you ask?

Well, if the guy was sitting down when you met him and it's one of your requirements that the guy to be taller than you, it makes sense to find some way of seeing how tall he is when he's standing up. It is better for you to find out now than to get to really like Hot Guy and then find out on the first date that he is four inches shorter than you. Some people may think it's kind of sneaky to do things like this. Their argument is that a relationship should just happen "naturally." But let's face it—everyone screens. All I suggest is screening as quickly as possible so your time (and his) doesn't get wasted.

Needless to say, the pool game goes well, and you have decided that you are starting to like this guy.

You have a choice now.

If you want, you can spend the evening hanging out with this guy. Or, you could set up a future meeting (i.e., Date #1). I think a lot of nonsense gets talked about cutting dates short and keeping the guy hanging on. Most of this comes from women trying to understand why that one date they had this month didn't work out—in other words, why the guy slept with them and then didn't call. They ask themselves questions like, "*Was it because I made it too easy? Did I call him too soon? Should I have waited till the third date?*" and then rack their brains trying to find an answer to the "*Why?*"

The truth is, if he didn't call you, he probably found you attractive enough to want to sleep with you once but he didn't want to date you. (That comes directly from guys I've interviewed. I'm not trying to be a bitch.)

If a guy likes you and wants to date you, it doesn't really make much difference if you play hard-to-get or not. He will still want to date you. However, if he thinks you are playing hard-to-get deliberately, he may get annoyed and move on.

In this situation, you decide you want to set up a meeting because you want to keep hanging with your friends, who have decided to move on to another bar.

YOU: It looks like my friends are moving on. I should get going.

HOT GUY: OK. Well, it's been a real pleasure meeting you. Let's exchange phone numbers.

YOU: Er . . . I'm not so big on phones. But what's your schedule like this week?

HOT GUY: Let me see. Tomorrow's no good, but I am around on Thursday. Could you do something then?

YOU: Sure—Thursday works.

HOT GUY: How about we go to dinner at that sushi place I was telling you about.

YOU: Sounds good. What time?

HOT GUY: Eight?

YOU: Sounds good. Shall we swap phone numbers just in case?

HOT GUY: OK. (Swap numbers.)

YOU: All right! So if I don't hear from you, I'll see you there at eight on Thursday!

HOT GUY: Cool. I look forward to it.

YOU: Me, too. Bye!

Notice how you've bypassed the whole tedious phone game. Now you and Hot Guy are going to continue your enjoyable conversation later in the week. If he can't make it for whatever reason, he'll definitely call. Given how well your initial interaction went, it's very unlikely that he will cancel.

The whole interaction probably took less than thirty minutes. There's no reason why you couldn't do this five times in one evening. And if these five guys ended up being guys that merited further exploration, that's five first dates a week from just one fun evening out.

Epilogue: Brilliant Concluding Thoughts

I BELIEVE THAT women as a whole have been misled: that's why I wrote this book. We have been misled by advice that is unconsciously based on the premise that decent men are hard to find. And when the "good ones" do come into our lives, it's a rare occurrence, so we had better not mess it up. Talk about pressure!

Fortunately, this advice is not true.

There are three things that come into play when molding your personal dating happiness:

1. **Up Your Numbers.**

    Dating is a numbers game. The more guys you meet, the greater the chance you have of finding the ones you hit it off with—"the good ones." This statement is not a new one. It has been part of the dating dogma for as long as people have been sexually attracted to one another. What is new is the knowledge that we, as women, now have a surefire way to meet the guys we are interested in meeting. We can talk to the guys we want to talk to, and we no longer have to rely on sifting through guys who definitely are not giving us the vibe that they fall into the "good ones" category.

With the knowledge I have shared in this book, it is entirely possible to meet ten new guys per night. Go out three nights per week, and that's thirty guys per week. Hit if off with one guy in a hundred, and you're meeting a "good one" roughly once every month, maybe more.

2. **Know Your List.**

Don't waste time on guys you don't want.

Use your List to screen the potential Hot Guys you've chosen to see if they are "good ones." You may be meeting thirty new guys per week, but without the knowledge of what works for you and what doesn't in a partner, those thirty guys are useless.

3. **Bring Enough to the Table.**

I was once at a party with my friend Ella. She was wearing a flannel shirt with a sexy tank top underneath and jeans. She wasn't a girly-girl and seldom followed fashion trends—although she always managed to look stellar no matter what she was wearing. Everyone else at the party was decked out in their sexiest party wear. A couple of the other girls were making snide remarks about her outfit, and after one particularly rude comment (which we ignored), I asked Ella if it bugged her that people talked about her that way.

Her reply to me was something I'll remember for the rest of my life.

She said, "Sam—it doesn't matter what you're wearing. It doesn't matter what you look like. It's about 'owning it.' If you rock what you're wearing, and you rock yourself—you'll be the sexiest girl in the room."

What she meant was that if I am confident in myself, then whatever I am wearing won't matter. My confidence will shine through, and I could be wearing a burlap bag and still be sexy. I adopted her philosophy, and the next time I felt like I was having a bad hair day or my shoes were totally wrong, I decided I would "own it" instead. And you know what? Before I knew it, I felt completely confident in myself and in my appearance.

My point here is that what matters the most is what you're packing on the inside. Your confidence is the sexiest and most attractive accessory of all. Whatever it is about you that makes you you—own it. Be proud. If you can believe in yourself and let the real you shine—not the you that you think others want to see, but the real, sexy, inner you—you'll always bring enough to the table.

Put all that together and you've got a surefire way to meet any guy, anytime, anywhere.

That's all there is to it. Go get 'em, tiger.

Appendix

Frequently Asked Questions

I received the following questions via email or from the women with whom I have shared my methods. I've selected the ones that popped up most often. If you think of any more, email me at sam@screwcupidthebook.com and I'll add them to a later version of this book.

Should I make eye contact before I approach?

Negative. Making eye contact constitutes flirting, and flirting translates to "I'm interested in you." Getting "accidental" proximity would be impossible if you had made eye contact with your target beforehand. He would know for sure that you didn't just "happen" to slide into the bar right next to him to get your drink. However, if no eye contact has been made before you get proximity and deliver your opener, there is no tip-off that you are interested in him. He may have noticed you and tried to make eye contact with you before this, but you will have been strong and not let on that you thought he was your kind of Hot Guy.

Note: checking him out when you are sure he's not looking to make sure he's cute is more than fine.

Is this something I can do alone?

By all means, YES!! As you probably noticed, some of the openers that I've given you require that you be with some friends to make sense. But you can adapt most of them to use by yourself. For example, you can say, "Help me out with something. I just got off the phone with a friend, and she says that blah blah blah."

Also, depending on your personality, you may prefer doing this by yourself. I personally find it can be a fun alternative to going out with my girlfriends. I feel like I have more freedom to cruise the room and talk to whomever I want. Plus, I tend to worry about whether my friend is enjoying herself when she's "taking one for the team" and talking to the less attractive friend of the Hot Guy I'm talking to.

If you have a free Tuesday evening, but none of your girlfriends is in the mood, just go out by yourself. If anyone asks where your friends are, just say they're "on their way." No one will be the wiser.

Does this only work at bars, or can I do this anywhere?

I've focused a lot on bars and clubs because they are such great places to meet people. You can go out with your friends, have a fun time, and meet great guys. Plus, there are lots of guys all in the same place, so you don't have to spend as much time looking for them. If it is a Friday or a

Saturday night, there is a good chance that the guys you meet will be single. And no one is in a hurry to get somewhere else because they are all out to socialize anyway. What's not to like?

However, bars are not for everyone. And that's fine. You can absolutely use these principles anywhere: bookstores, coffee shops, on the street, in the park, on the beach, at the driving range—pretty much anywhere you feel safe and where there are good-looking guys is fair game.

I just walked up to this guy and used one of your openers, and it was really awkward. What did I do wrong?

If you just "walked up to a guy," chances are you may need a little help getting proximity. Just walking up to someone directly conveys interest. He knew you were interested before you even started talking, which is not neutral. You need a natural way to get near someone, with an obvious other reason why you are there besides him. In bars, get a drink or be on your way to the jukebox. In coffee shops, be on your way to the bathroom or sit near the guy you want to talk to with your newspaper. In any store, just pretend to be totally interested in whatever product is near him. On the street (or in a mall or wherever) it is fine to stop someone and open them, but you need to be walking near them beforehand.

I have a crush on my coworker's friend. We've been introduced a couple of times, but he seemed kind of quiet. Since I already know him, as an acquaintance, how do I start a conversation with him? Your advice is based purely on how to approach someone you don't know at all.

This is not nearly as tricky as it might seem. I know what you mean about some of the openers assuming no knowledge about the Hot Guy and therefore not being the best choices for someone you're acquainted with. However, some of the other more "I have a question I desperately need answered" openers will work just fine. Let me show you:

YOU: Hi! I think we've met a couple of times—you're [insert coworker's name here]'s friend right?

HIM: Yeah. You're [insert your name], right?

YOU: Yep, that's me! Can I ask you a question? I just got off the phone with my girlfriend, and we're utterly perplexed. She went on a date last week with this dude, and it went well. He called today and left her a voice mail that said "Had fun, see you around." What does that mean in guyspeak? Should she call him back?

HIM: I'd say he's playing it cool. If he was desperate to see her again, he would have asked her out again.

YOU: Huh. Do you think she should call him?

HIM: If she wants to—as long as she realizes that it's possible he's not that into it. You sound dubious—do you think she should call him?

Now they've got a conversation going and it should be relatively easy to segue into another topic—movies, thoughts on good restaurants (starting with the one the friend went to on her date, perhaps?), travel, and so forth.

I made up an opener, but it didn't work. I said, "Hey—can I get your opinion on something? What do you think of Sheryl Crow?"

This is nearly a good opener, but the problem is the subcommunication. Why do you care what he thinks of Sheryl Crow?

The subcommunication you are making here is "You look like someone I'd like to know. I'd like to know what you think of Sheryl Crow." Asking someone's opinion is not by itself neutral. It becomes neutral when you give them a reason for wanting their opinion that has nothing to do with them.

You could turn this into a workable opener by saying, "Hey—can I get your opinion on something? My friends and I are arguing about Sheryl Crow. One of my friends says that guys don't like her music. But that's bullshit, right? Can you help me talk some sense into her?" Now you want his opinion to help you with an argument. You're not asking because you have decided you like him and want to get to know him. This is subtle, but it will make all the difference.

What if I don't like him?

This happens. You get close enough to him to really see his true colors, and he is not as cute as you thought. Or he says something that makes you wince internally and you figure out he is definitely not the guy for you. If this happens, bail on the interaction ASAP. Just say brightly, "Thanks for your help on my dilemma (or whatever it was that you opened him with). It was nice meeting you—bye!" and eject. Think no more about it. Not every guy you meet is going to be cool.

I made up a poker opener: "My friends and I were arguing: Does a flush beat a straight, or is it the other way around?" but I can't get it to work. What am I doing wrong?

This is maybe salvageable as an opener, provided you have something strong that you can lead into afterward. Otherwise, the guy is just going to say, "A flush beats a straight" or "I don't know," and then that's the end of your conversation.

If you have a good follow-up to this opener, you might get away with it. However, the real problem is that your question is not really a matter of opinion; it is just a factual question that the guy either knows the answer to or doesn't. It works much better to have questions that require opinions as responses. It makes the conversation more interesting, the guy will talk for longer than if he were just settling a fact for you, and it gives you something to bust on him with.

I don't get this whole "making up openers" thing. What advice can you give me?

When you are thinking up your own openers, remember that whatever you ask the guy needs to be something that he will know the answer to. You cannot, for example, expect a guy to know the latest fashions on the runway, or why so-and-so was on the cover of that magazine *again*. There are millions of things that "guys" would stereotypically know the answer to. Use the stereotypes to your advantage. Sports, beer, poker, why-guys-act-the-way-they-do, and tools are all good bets for openers.

On that same note, asking a guy something that he can be knowledgeable about plays on the damsel–in-distress scenario. Guys like feeling that they know more than you do. It makes them feel powerful. And though I am definitely not advocating dumbing yourself down to get a guy, it doesn't really matter if you know the answer to the question or not. Guys like to help girls—it makes them feel macho.

Also, it is good to try to make statements that invite further conversation rather than a simple yes or no. That way, the guy feels like he is doing the work and cleverly coming up with conversation based on what you are saying. He feels like he is hitting on you rather than vice versa. Example: "You guys look like you've been playing tennis awhile" rather than "Have you guys been playing tennis awhile?"

Don't you get nervous?

Definitely. The good news is that the more you do this, the less nervous you will become. I still get butterflies occasionally. I just need to psych myself up beforehand so that I'm in the right mental state for delivering my opener. Opening a Hot Guy is a very similar experience to public speaking for me. I get nervous, and I get butterflies. I sometimes even do that slight nervous sweat thing, but once I'm in, I'm totally fine. I've gotten to the point now where I love the nerves—they keep me sharp, and the rush is great.

Additionally, if you think about how these openers are staged, it would be natural for you to be a bit nervous—you are asking a random stranger for advice, after all. So if you feel nervous, let it show a little bit. I find it works best when I don't stare at the guy the whole time. I also look up or down when I'm "thinking" about something, like their response. You want to make this as realistic as possible. If you're starting to talk too fast (or too low) for them to understand you, or you're stuttering or fidgeting or otherwise conveying that you are freaked out, you may want to practice a bit more. Otherwise, he'll wonder what's up.

What do I do if it doesn't work?

Sometimes it won't work. You are learning, and you will make mistakes. Just remember that dating is a numbers game. And now that you have the power to talk to anyone you want, if one opener gets screwed up, it does not matter in the slightest. There are hundreds more guys where he came from. If you mess up an opener, rather than getting bummed out, think of it as having gained some knowledge about where your potential hang-ups are.

Why can't I just walk up and say "Hi"?

Saying "Hi" forces a split-second decision from the guy about you. This is because saying "Hi" is what we say when what we really mean is "You're hot, and I want to date you." It doesn't work very often (and believe me, I've tried). Why? Because I have given those guys two seconds to decide how they are going to respond—and most guys make their decision about a girl in the first half second if she makes it obvious she likes him. Since my value was already decreased because I had "hit on him," my odds sucked for success. It may work sometimes, but it's not a reliable way to open a communication with someone.

Why can't I just walk up and say, "Nice shoes. Wanna fuck?"

See "Why can't I just walk up and say 'Hi'?" The difference is that this falls into the cheesy pickup-line category. The only situation in which I have ever seen this one work (in girl-on-guy pickup) is when the girl said it as a joke—in other words, she may have liked him but was using the cheesy line to get a laugh.

I think you're crazy. Girls shouldn't approach guys. Haven't you read The Rules?

Hopefully by now, I've laid out my side of the argument thoroughly enough that you aren't still thinking this. However, if you still feel this way, email me at sam@screwcupidthebook.com. I'll buy you a drink and show you how it works in person. You won't regret it, I promise.

How many nights a week do I need to go out to make this work?

I'm assuming by "making this work" you are referring to "meeting people you like."

Meeting people you like is entirely a numbers game. The more people you come into contact with, the more likely it is that you will find people you like. Period.

As for the number of nights per week? It depends totally on how focused you are. If you go out with the goal of meeting ten new guys every time you go out, going out three times a week will put you in contact with thirty guys. If I apply my theory that I have the "click factor" with one out of every hundred guys, it's only going to take me a month to meet someone I click with, statistically speaking.

What do I do if I can tell he's not into me?

If you sense that the conversation is not going well, you can bail at any point. You can keep your dignity intact by just saying, "Thanks for your input—that's really helped me out."

If at any point the guy thought that you might have been hitting on him, this will completely negate that conclusion. You just left the conversation, and you would not have done that if you were into him.

I think you are full of it and are just giving women false hope. And that's really messed up—you're just going to be making women more depressed about the dating situation out there.

First off, I am sorry you feel so negative about the dating world. But I did not write this book to depress people further. I wrote it to give women a way to take control of their dating lives.

It's a common story: Girls start off thinking that guys are hard to meet, and they feel lonely and sad; they feel like failures. Some will stop exercising, sit at home, and begin the downward slide. My aim here is to provide a solution, not add to the misery.

What is the point of someone with that mind-set taking care of herself if she can only meet one or two guys a year? My aim is to motivate girls and give them the hope that there *are* people out there they can actually meet and get dates with. Maybe it is tough, but it is worlds better than the patronizing, feel-good-with-no-viable-solution advice out there. I hope that these strategies give the women you describe the drive to help themselves.

What do I do if he's wearing headphones and can't hear me when I talk to him?

Hmmm. I would decide whether or not to approach him on a case-by-case basis. For example, if he's wearing headphones and his eyes are shut, he's pretty strongly indicating that he doesn't want to be bothered. He's closed off sight and sound to the outside world—those are two pretty major senses to cut off. If, however, he's got headphones in and his eyes are open, I think it's OK to tap him on the shoulder and deliver your opener. You may occasionally get an annoyed reaction, but most guys will be fine with it.

How do I talk to the Hot Guy I've seen a bunch of times before in the gym or coffee shop or wherever—and it's clear we recognize each other because we've exchanged smiles—but we've never spoken. It seems like it might be awkward to treat him like a guy I've never seen.

This is a great question. However, I disagree that it would be awkward to open him normally. If there have been smiles or at least acknowledgment that you two recognize each other and he hasn't spoken to you yet, he'll probably be stoked that you're initiating conversation, so if anything, this particular Hot Guy will be even easier to open than normal because he's more likely to be receptive right off the bat. That said, bringing up that you've seen him around could be construed as sexual interest, which as you know you always want to avoid when first opening a Hot Guy—so I would avoid that. I recommend treating him like every other guy you open. Start with an "Excuse me, can I ask you a question?" and go into your chosen opener. One of the ones about "I just got off the phone with my girlfriend and she was wondering what guys mean when they say 'See you around'" or whether she should call a guy when he hasn't responded to her text is good. These are a bit more "I have a spur-of-the-moment question that needs answering," and will definitely appear neutral.

More Examples of Openers

The examples I have listed here all follow the same basic formula. This formula is completely based on using a neutral approach: first you get proximity, then you get into the right mental place, then you deliver the opener, then you follow up.

The openers listed here are all ones I have used myself, so you can be assured that they do indeed work.

You can play with the actual words in the openers and make them your own. After all, it's a lot easier to get into the frame of wondering something enough to want to know a guy's opinion on it if you are actually wondering about that thing. I give you these as a guideline. Feel free to add to, delete from, or create new ones as you see fit.

You'll note that for most of the guy's responses to these openers, I've put "blah blah blah." This is because I want to emphasize that it doesn't matter what the guy says in response. Your objective when you open Hot Guy is to have an opener and two or three follow-up things you can say, regardless of what Hot Guy says back to you. If he says something that is easy to respond to, then by all means follow his conversational thread. But for the cases where he doesn't say anything useful that can be used to continue the conversation, you don't want to stall and get stuck saying, "Uh . . ." Since you have no idea whether the guy will be a conversationalist before you approach him, it is necessary to have two or three things planned out ahead of time.

• • •

Bar Openers

▶ Clint Eastwood opener

YOU: Guys—can you explain something to me? How come all guys think Clint Eastwood is so great? My roommate (or whoever) just made me sit through some lame-ass Western, and it was just dull. I mean, all he does is just narrow his eyes and talk in a husky voice, and everyone thinks he's so cool. What is that?

THEM: Blah blah blah. He's totally cool. Blah blah blah.

YOU: How come guys always have this man-crush on him?

THEM: Blah blah blah.

YOU: OK—what about Bruce Willis? Because I think he's pretty cool. Plus, he has the added bonus of actually being able to act.

THEM: Blah blah. *Die Hard*. Blah blah blah.

YOU: OK—What't the best action movie ever made?

THEM: Blah blah blah.

YOU: You have to be kidding! Blah blah blah was much better.

THEM: Blah blah blah.

▶ Bob Dylan opener

(Or whatever artist you don't like. I happen not to enjoy Bob Dylan's singing style, although I concede that his songwriting skills

are superior to most. Using Bob Dylan works very well in this opener, because I've never met a guy who doesn't like him. It always starts a conversation.)

YOU: Guys. Tell me something. How come guys think that Bob Dylan is good? My friends and I were just driving here, and they were playing a song on the radio in the car, and it was this whiny out-of-tune voice and this crappy harmonica playing, and the DJs are like, "Awesome song. Bob Dylan is the best." How can they say that? Is it like some joke and everyone actually thinks that he stinks? What is that?

GUYS: Blah blah blah. No way. Bob Dylan wrote blah blah blah. He's cool. Blah blah blah.

YOU: He wrote that? OK, well, then I admit he's a good songwriter, but as a musician, no way. Just so I can get an idea of where your music tastes lie so that I know how credible your opinions are, who are your top five bands?

GUYS: Blah blah blah.

(Note: the "so that I know how credible your opinions are, who are your top five" can be used with almost anything in the entertainment industry. It's a great lead into further conversation.)

▶ Text Message opener

YOU: Hey, can I ask you a question? I was just talking to my girlfriend, and she said that she texted the guy she went out with last week, but he hasn't responded yet. Should she call him? We'd love a guy opinion.

HIM: How many days has it been?

YOU: I think four days since their date. Why?

HIM: Well, I would say that she shouldn't call him until at least a week has passed. If he hasn't called or texted back by then, then it's OK to call once. But honestly, if he hasn't called her, he might not.

YOU: Interesting. I'll pass that along, thanks. I've got to say, I love texting as a quick alternative to email or a phone call, but it can get frustrating if people don't respond. How else do you know they got it?

HIM: Totally. Blah blah blah.

Soccer/Football [depending on location] opener

YOU: Can I ask you something?

HIM: Sure, what's up?

YOU: So my guy friends and I were talking, and they were saying that girls who know about soccer aren't cute. I'm not seeing the correlation. Is that a guy thing—to think that girls who like soccer aren't cute?

HIM: Ha-ha. No, I have no idea what they are talking about. Maybe they were just messing with you. Do you like soccer?

YOU: Actually, yes. I grew up around boys, and it was kind of inevitable, I guess. Maybe they were messing . . . huh. Do you like soccer, or are you an alternative sport kind of guy?

HIM: Blah blah blah.

▶ The Beer opener

YOU: Sorry to bother you, but can I ask you a guy question?

HIM: Shoot.

YOU: So, the new guy my friend is dating invited her over to hang out with him and his buddies—all of whom are guys. We've been racking our brains trying to come up with the perfect beer for her to bring. We thought Guinness, but fifty percent of the population doesn't like Guinness. Is there a beer that all guys are going to like?

HIM: Fifty percent of the population doesn't like Guinness? Wow. News to me. OK—yeah, blah blah blah.

YOU: Really? You think they'll all like that one?

HIM: Totally. It's not too dark, it's not too light. They'll love you forever.

YOU: What about bringing homemade cookies? We both thought that guys would definitely dig homemade goods, but we were worried that Tommy would think she was trying to hard. . . .

HIM: Trying too hard? My god—if someone made me cookies, I'd ask them to marry me.

YOU: Ha-ha. Marry you? You're that easy, huh?

HIM: Blah blah blah.

The "Date" opener

YOU: Can I ask you a guy question?

HIM: Sure. Go for it.

YOU: So, my girlfriend is going to "hang out" with this guy. He's kind of a friend of ours, so I guess we aren't even sure if it's a date or not, but he told her to pick the place. We're not sure where she should take him. We thought a restaurant would be too lovey-dovey, and she doesn't want to scare him off, so we thought a sports bar for a beer would be good. If a girl said "sports bar for a beer," would you think she was into you?

HIM: Blah blah blah.

YOU: Do you know of any good sports bars she could take him around here?

HIM: Yeah, there's one on Fourth that's cool. She could also take him to a movie—that's pretty low-key.

YOU: Really? It seemed too datelike to us. What movie, if you were the guy, would you want to see right now?

him: Blah blah blah.

Other Places

When He Has a Dog (No, you don't need one!)

YOU: Hey, that's a beautiful dog—what breed is it? (or, if the breed is obvious: "How old is she?")

HIM: Blah blah blah.

YOU: Hey, can you explain something to me? How come small dogs always shake? Why are they doing it? Are they scared, or cold, or what?

HIM: Blah blah blah.

At the Mall

YOU: Can I ask you something? Do you know if there is a sporting goods store around here? I'm trying to find a place to buy a (volleyball/basketball/soccer ball).

HIM: Yeah, there's one on Twenty-sixth.

YOU: Cool, thanks—I'm taking a class on Monday nights to relearn the ropes, but I want to practice during the week. Do you play?

HIM: Yeah, I play with the city league on the weekends.

YOU: Wow, you must be really good. You would know where I can go to practice then, no?

HIM: Blah blah blah.

At the Swimming Pool

YOU: Hey—can you explain something to me? I was swimming laps just now, and this guy grabs my foot while I'm swimming. I know sometimes people tap your foot to let you know they're passing, but grabbing it?

HIM: Yeah—he shouldn't have grabbed it.

YOU: I was like, "What the hell is that, grabbing my foot?" Has anyone ever grabbed your foot?

HIM: Heh-heh—no. That's never happened to me.

YOU: It's funny, I've always thought of this pool as being really friendly, but that's kind of weird for someone to do that. How do you think this pool compares with other ones?

HIM: Blah blah blah.

On the Beach

YOU: Excuse me—do you think I could I borrow some sunscreen? I totally forgot mine, and I'm sure I'm going to get fried.

HIM: Sure, here you go.

YOU: Thanks. By the way, do you know if there's somewhere around here I can take surfing lessons? I've been meaning to learn for a while, and I've finally got some free time coming up.

HIM: Blah blah blah.

YOU: I've often wondered—how can you tell where the waves are going to break?

HIM: Blah blah blah.

YOU: You seem like quite the surfer. Have you been surfing long?

▶ On the Tennis Courts
[just as Hot Guy has finished a game]

YOU: Excuse me, can you show me the right grip for serving? You looked pretty consistent out there.

HIM: Yeah, you hold it like this. Blah blah blah.

YOU: You know, I've been playing tennis for over a year, and I guess I've been hitting it wrong all this time. You guys look like you've been playing a while.

HIM: Blah blah blah.

▶ At the Sailing Club

YOU: Can I ask you something? Do you think it's wrong to be hanging out at with a sailing club if you've never been on a boat? My girlfriend asked me to come along tonight to keep her company, but I feel like a bit of a fraud.

HIM: Of course it's OK. We love new people.

YOU: So, I take it you've been on a boat before?

HIM: Blah blah blah. Yeah, my yacht is in the harbor, blah blah blah.

YOU: Have you ever sailed to somewhere other than the U.S.? I've always thought that would be cool.

HIM: Blah blah blah.

▶ At the Charity Fund-raiser

YOU: [Turning to your target as if the thought just struck you.] Wasn't that an interesting speech by blah blah blah?

HIM: Blah blah blah.

YOU: Can I ask you a question? Did you think the speaker maybe had a bit of an agenda (if the speaker seemed to have an agenda)? Sometimes I find at these things that the speaker seems to have an agenda, but I didn't get that feeling with this speaker. Did you (if the speaker didn't seem to have an agenda)?

HIM: Blah blah blah.

YOU: So, what brings you here, anyway?

HIM: Blah blah blah.

On a Hike #1

[Guys are coming toward you, having already been to the destination while you are on your way there.]

YOU: Hey, guys, is it much further to the summit?

THEM: Blah blah blah.

YOU: What is there to see? Is it worth seeing?

THEM: Blah blah blah.

YOU: We went hiking a couple of weeks ago to blah blah blah. It was awesome! Have you been there yet?

THEM: Blah blah blah.

YOU: Do you know of any decent hiking groups? Some of them scare us because the people are pretty intense, but we are looking for a group of cool people to go hiking with.

THEM: Blah blah blah.

On a Hike #2

[You've been to the destination and are coming back down. They are coming toward you on their way there. It's only another mile to the summit, but you tease them a bit.]

YOU: Guys, you do realize you have about another twelve miles to the summit, right?

THEM: Yeah, right. We've done this hike before. Blah blah blah.

YOU: No, they've moved it. It's much farther now.

THEM: Uh-huh. Blah blah blah.

YOU: Actually, in all seriousness—it's stunning up there. The sun was shining off the waterfall and casting rainbows everywhere. It's awesome. It reminded me a little of the blah blah blah hike. Have you guys been there yet?

THEM: Blah blah blah.

YOU: Actually, do you know of any decent hiking groups? Some of them scare us because the people are pretty intense, but we are looking for a group of cool people to go hiking with.

THEM: Blah blah blah.

At Your Ski Club Kickoff Party

YOU: OK, guys—tell me something. . . .

THEM: OK . . .

YOU: So, my guy friends and I were having this argument before I came here tonight—I was trying to understand how come guys always need a beer in their hands to enjoy watching professional sports? What is it with guys, sports, and beer?

THEM: Blah blah blah.

YOU: Are guys born with some signal that fires off in their brains when they watch a game that says "I NEED BEER"? What's the deal with that?

THEM: Blah blah blah.

YOU: What about watching golf—that doesn't cause quite as much of a ruckus as football or soccer—why don't people drink so much beer when they're watching golf?

THEM: Blah blah blah.

▶ ## At (the End of) Your Yoga/Pilates/Spinning Class

YOU: Wow—I forgot how intense that class is. Last time I came, I guess I was more in shape! Is (he/she) the usual instructor, do you know?

HIM: Yes, as far as I know.

YOU: When I came to these classes before, there was a guy who taught them who I swear was a sadist. We got a good workout, but somehow I came away feeling abused. You ever feel like that?

HIM: (laughing) Blah blah blah.

YOU: I still haven't figured out if it's the class I enjoy or if it's the triumphant feeling I get by getting through the class that I like more. . . .

HIM: Blah blah blah.

YOU: Are you coming down just to stay in shape, or do you have some other goal in mind?

HIM: Blah blah blah.

In the DMV Waiting Area (Or Anywhere You're Forced to Fill Out Lots of Paperwork)

[Just don't pick up a pen. Then sit near the guy you want to meet.]

YOU: Excuse me—do you have a pen I could borrow?

(Answer #1) HIM: Sure . . . here you go.

(Answer #2) HIM: No, but they have some over there.

YOU: Thanks. . . . Filling in these things always reminds me of exams—like we're going to get graded on them or something. . . . What are you in here for?

HIM: Blah blah blah.

YOU: I have to renew my driver's license. I keep getting flashbacks to my first driving test. I think I actually failed to come to a complete stop at a stop sign, but he still passed me. Do you think girls get away with stuff because they're girls?

HIM: Blah blah blah.

At the Farmer's/Outdoor Market

YOU: Sorry to bother you, but can I ask you something? I need a guy's opinion on something.

HIM: Sure.

YOU: Have you ever cooked dinner for someone?

HIM: Blah blah blah.

YOU: My friend and I were talking about this earlier today. This new guy she's seeing made her lamb chops the other night, and she thinks that because he did that, he's totally into her. Is there a meal that guys will make when they are totally into you, or is it just that he liked lamb?

HIM: Blah blah blah.

YOU: What about lasagna? Is that a "good sign" meal?

HIM: Blah blah blah.

YOU: Speaking of lasagna, have you tried that Italian restaurant on Sixth and Broadway? It's to die for.

HIM: Blah blah blah.

At a Restaurant—#1

[When you arrive at a restaurant, rather than accepting the first table you are offered, subtly figure out if there are any cute guys there, and, if so, ask if you can have the table that happens to be next to them. Once you're settled in . . .]

YOU: Hey, guys, we're sorry to break in on you, but since you're male, we were hoping you could settle an argument for us.

THEM: Blah blah blah. Sure.

YOU: Cool. So, my friend here thinks that the three-day rule in the movie *Swingers* is BS. She thinks it's OK to call a guy the next day and that rules like that are lame. I agree they're lame but think that it's necessary to play by them if you want a call back. So, our question to you is: Rules or no?

THEM: Blah blah blah.

YOU: Well, have you ever gotten a callback by calling the day after you meet them? I mean, that scene where Jon Favreau calls that girl about fifteen times is excruciating because it's so realistic.

THEM: Blah blah blah.

YOU: Have you seen the rest of the Vince Vaughn movies—like the ones he's done with Owen Wilson and Will Ferrell? They're hysterical.

THEM: Blah blah blah.

▶ At a Restaurant—#2

[If you are already seated and a group of cute guys arrives and gets seated three tables away, it might be a bit challenging. However, if you are really ballsy, you could stop on the way back from the bathroom and say . . .]

YOU: Hey, guys, I'm sorry to break in on you, but we really need a male opinion on something. We have this girlfriend, and she insists on calling guys by a pet name—like from about the second date onward. The guys get freaked out very soon afterward, and we think that's why. It would weird you out if a girl had a pet name for you already by the second date, right?

THEM: Blah blah blah.

YOU: The last pet name my friend used on a guy was "Tarzan." We think it just made the guy uncomfortable—he wasn't even that buff. Have you guys ever been called a pet name that didn't weird you out, or that you actually liked, that I can suggest as an alternative? We don't think we can stop her from doing it, but at least we can maybe get her to use something acceptable.

THEM: Blah blah blah. Super King. Blah blah blah.

YOU: Are you serious? Ha-ha. I'll pass that on.

THEM: Blah blah blah.

YOU: Hey, did you guys eat anything good?

THEM: Blah blah blah.

In the Golf Course Parking Lot

YOU: Can I ask you something?

HIM: Sure.

YOU: Maybe this is overly petty of me or something—I'd be interested to get someone else's opinion on it. So, we were getting held up quite a lot by this group of four in front of us, and on the fourteenth hole, one of them hit a ball into the trees and spent twenty minutes looking for it before giving up and taking the drop. Now, I've always been taught that if you're holding up play that much, you should let the people behind through. They didn't seem to know about this, but do you think that's something most people do, or am I just being petty?

HIM: Blah blah blah.

YOU: Thanks. It was just a small thing—I didn't want to make a big deal of it. I actually had a great round. How did you do?

HIM: Blah blah blah.

YOU: This is one of my favorite courses. I also like blah blah blah. Have you played over there?

HIM: Blah blah blah.

▶ At the Driving Range

YOU: Excuse me—can I ask you something?

HIM: Sure.

YOU: I've been watching your shots, and you seem to hit it pretty straight every time. I occasionally hit a killer drive, but I'm not consistent at all. Is there a trick to getting it so consistent?

HIM: Blah blah blah.

YOU: Have you played on the course here? Is it easy or hard, would you say?

HIM: Blah blah blah.

YOU: Where else have you played around here?

HIM: Blah blah blah.

At That Hip New Gallery Opening

YOU: Can I ask you a question?

HIM: Sure. Ask away.

YOU: OK, I know I should be thinking about the art, and there's some really cool stuff here, but I keep thinking about this thing that happened on the way here. So, I saw this guy in his convertible with the top down, and he was singing along to that song "Sometimes when we touch, the honesty's too much"—and it was really weird—seriously, I mean, I know the song, but I'd never sing along to it. Isn't that weird?

HIM: Blah blah blah.

YOU: But the most annoying thing is that now I have that song stuck in my head, but I don't know what the next line is so I just kind of go, "And I have to hmmm hmm hmmm hmm hmm." I don't want to offend you by presuming that you know the song, but do you know how it goes after that?

HIM: Blah blah blah.

At a Rock Concert

YOU: Can I tell you a secret? I can never go to a concert without thinking of that scene from *Wayne's World* where they get passed around on top of the crowd at that Alice Cooper concert. It's always been a secret wish of mine to do that. Do people really do that?

HIM: Blah blah blah.

YOU: What about stage diving? I always thought you could get hurt doing that.

HIM: Blah blah blah.

YOU: So, have you seen these guys before?

HIM: Blah blah blah.

At the Gym

[Be sensitive to the Hot Guy's schedule. He may be taking a precise time, such as one or two minutes, between sets. If this is the case, break up the conversation into chunks. The conversation then turns into kind of a running joke.]

YOU: You want to know something messed up? Last time I was here, there was this guy grunting so loudly that I could hardly keep from laughing. He was making these "nggaaaahh" sounds. Oh my god—I could hardly control myself. Why do guys do that?

HIM: Blah blah blah.

YOU: You don't do that, do you? You're not a grunter, are you?

HIM: Blah blah blah.

[Then, whenever you run into each other later in your session at the gym, you can do silly grunt sounds at each other and have an inside joke. When his session is over, you can ask him something simple like, "So, how often do you work out?" and continue the conversation you started.]

When He's on the Bicycle Next to You at a Stop Light

[Make sure you've timed it so you've got more than 10 seconds to talk. Preferably, time it so that you end up next to him just as the light turns red.]

YOU: Excuse me—can I ask you something?

HIM: Sure!

YOU: I've just started riding my bike around the city [or, if you've been riding your bike for a while, you could say "this route" or "this part of the city"]—is there a good place around here to stop for a drink that has a bike rack?

HIM: Yep! Blah blah blah.

YOU: Great! Thanks. I'm thinking about getting into the amateur racing circuit on the weekends but don't know where to start. Do you know of any groups I can talk to? [or, if he doesn't look like he's into the competitive side of the sport] I'm looking to upgrade my tires/seat/handlebars/etc. Do you know of a good place?

HIM: Blah blah blah.

▶ At a Soccer/Basketball/Football/Baseball/Rugby/Whatever Game—#1

[If the guys are in their seats and near enough to you that you can talk naturally]

YOU: Guys, can you explain something to me? What happens at the end of the game if the score is the same? Is it just a tie?

THEM: Blah blah blah.

YOU: So, who's going to be winning? (or, if it's obvious—"Do you think [the losing team] have a chance?")

THEM: Blah blah blah.

[Then . . . wait for a break in the action, such as at half- or quartertime. Guys will be annoyed to be pestered too much during the game.]

YOU: OK, I see what you guys mean. Looks like [the winning team] have it, right?

THEM: Blah blah blah.

YOU: So, do you come to these games a lot?

At a Soccer/Basketball/Football/Baseball/ Rugby/Whatever Game—#2

[If the guys are not comfortably near you, wait for the break and when the guy you like gets up, follow him (subtly, of course). He's probably gone to get some food—guys always do. When he stops moving, just get proximity.]

YOU: Hey, what's good to eat here? Are the hot dogs any good?

HIM: Blah blah blah.

YOU: A friend of mine said I should try the Dodger Dog [or whatever]. Are they good?

HIM: Blah blah blah.

YOU: Hey, can you explain something to me? [Now, just go into the "what happens at the end of the game?" conversation.]

At the Video Store

YOU: Excuse me . . . have you seen *Alien* or *Predator*? It's definitely an action movie night for me, and I haven't seen either one.

HIM: Blah blah blah.

YOU: Yeah, my friends said they were both good, but I'm wondering which one to get.

HIM: Blah blah blah.

YOU: A friend of mine made me watch Running Man the other day, and I didn't think too much of it. Just so I can calibrate your advice, what did you think of it?

At the Magazine Stand

YOU: [reading a magazine] Do you think it's kind of messed up to come into a store and read a whole magazine and then not buy it?

HIM: Blah blah blah.

YOU: A friend of mine comes in here all the time and reads the whole magazine through, whereas I get guilt pangs if I read more than a few pages.

HIM: Blah blah blah.

YOU: What about downloading songs? Do you think that's OK?

HIM: Blah blah blah.

In a Coffee Shop

YOU: Can I ask you something? Do you think it's wrong not to call a guy back? I went on a date about a week ago, and the guy was OK, but I just don't think I want to see him again. But he's been calling me quite a lot—do you think it's wrong to just ignore him?

HIM: Blah blah blah.

YOU: OK, so my friend made out with this guy once and then didn't call him. Now, I think that's wrong, right? Because he must be wondering what happened.

HIM: Blah blah blah.

YOU: What do you say to a girl if it's not really on between you?

HIM: Blah blah blah.

YOU: Oooh, that's good. I could use that. Actually, it's a shame because although the date was no good, we went to this really cool bar [then just name a cool bar near you that he's probably heard of]. Do you know it?

HIM: Blah blah blah.

Anywhere—#1

YOU: Can I ask you something? Do you find that when you have a friend you spend a lot of time with and they move away, you see their face everywhere? It's as if you're expecting them to still be around, even though you know they're not. Do you think that's odd?

HIM: Blah blah blah. Who do you keep seeing around?

YOU: She was my roommate in college, and I know her like a sister. It's weird now that she's not here. Do you know what I'm talking about? Has that ever happened to you?

HIM: Blah blah blah.

▶ Anywhere—#2

YOU: Hey, guys, can I ask you a question? I'm worried about a friend of mine. I just got off the phone with her, and she says that her boyfriend thinks they should spend more time apart. He doesn't want to break up or anything; he just thinks they spend too much time together. Is that weird? I'd be interested in a guy's perspective.

THEM: Blah blah blah.

YOU: He definitely doesn't want to break up with her, and I'm pretty sure he doesn't want to see other girls. He just feels cramped. Does that happen to guys more than it happens to girls?

THEM: Blah blah blah.

▶ Anywhere—#3

[This one works when they are wearing something that you genuinely admire and want to know where they got it so you can buy it for yourself.]

YOU: I'm sorry, but can I ask you where you got your messenger bag/shoes/bike/etc.?

HIM: Sure! Blah blah blah.

YOU: Thanks so much. I really dig it. [Then, insert one of the following questions, depending on what he said.] Did they have others like it?/How long ago did you buy it?/Any complaints about it?

HIM: Blah blah blah.

YOU: Thanks, you've been a big help. I love finding a new awesome thing like that to hunt down. Have you ever been to [insert cool store or cool website here]? They've always got something unique and cool.

HIM: Blah blah blah.

▶ Blind Date opener

[This example is a little different. It shows how you can be creative and try new things out, provided you stick to the basic principles of a neutral opener. It's one of my favorites because you get to act a bit, which is always fun.

Go into a bar. Look around subtly to see if there is anyone you like. If you see someone, go and take a seat near him (or stand near him if there are no seats). You don't want to be unnaturally near—just put yourself within normal proximity.]

YOU: (Pretend to be waiting for a blind date. Check your watch repeatedly and look at every person who comes through the door in addition to scanning the room repeatedly. Look at your target every ten seconds or so. Let this go on for about forty seconds. He may be a little weirded out that you keep staring at him. Check your watch, scan the room, sigh, and then look at him again.) Excuse me, I'm sorry to keep looking at you, but is your name Mike?

HIM: Ah, no. Why?

YOU: (looking sheepish) Well, I'm here on a blind date, and he was supposed to be here ten minutes ago. How much longer do you think I should wait? I've never gone on a blind date before. I don't know how long you're supposed to wait.

HIM: (laughing) A blind date, huh? Do you know what he looks like?

YOU: Ermph, no. I met him on the Internet, actually (sheepish grin); he *said* he was six-two, brown hair, blue eyes, tan—you know, the standard Internet profile (look at watch again). I think I'm entering stood-up territory.

HIM: Hmmmm. Well, my friend and I are just having an after-work drink . . . you're already here; why don't you join us? If he shows, hopefully he matches his profile. If not? Well, we're both six-two, and I have brown hair.

YOU: (laughing) Sounds like a plan. Where do you work?

Glossary

BLOWN OFF: What occurs to the unfortunate person who receives an icy shoulder when attempting to make contact with a target. *Brandon approached the blonde with a swagger, leaned in, and said, "Hey, baby. Can I buy you a drink?" He was immediately* **blown off** *by the blonde, who had correctly translated his question into the true inquiry it was: "Can I have sex with you?"* (Page 35)

BODY LANGUAGE: The subcommunication one makes to a Hot Guy with one's movements, tone, eyes, position when standing or sitting, etc. *Although Katie's conversation was neutral, her* **body language** *was anything but: it was abundantly clear to anyone watching the exchange between her and Brent that Katie was very interested in him, largely because she had one hand firmly planted on this thigh.* (Pages 40, 44, 79–80)

BUSTING/CALIBRATED TEASING: Teasing lightly (in good humor) as a form of flirting. This takes practice, but the skill is an excellent one for picking up Hot Guys. *Jane was constantly busting on her friend Dave for being such a computer geek.* (Page 77)

CELL PHONE: A prop used when picking up Hot Guys. You can pretend to check your messages while meandering innocently into the vicinity of the chosen Hot Guy. They are also occasionally useful for making phone calls. *Even though I just accidentally dropped my **cell phone** in my glass of water, I'm going to dry it off, pretend it still works, and "check my messages" as I wander over near that Hot Guy.* (Pages 44, 48, 83)

CLICK FACTOR: That feeling you get when you meet another person and you know that he understands you completely. If the **click factor** is there, thoughts are finished by the opposite party within the first ten minutes. This person is also someone you like immensely. *In other circles, the **click factor** could be synonymous with a soul mate.* (Pages 84–85, 87–88, 90)

COMBINING OPENERS: The action of stringing together two or more openers. This is used when the Hot Guy is less than enthusiastic about responding. *When James didn't respond to Bridget, she immediately **combined openers** by busting out her killer beer opener.* (Pages 74–75)

CONDOM: What should always be in your purse and what should always be worn. For example, this phrase should never be uttered: *We don't have a **condom**? That's OK, I'm invincible.* (Page 83)

CONVERSATION PIECE (noun): A piece of clothing or jewelry that is interesting and/or outrageous, so as to elicit comments from those who view it. *Although Bianca felt that wearing a necklace made of dryer lint to be at the height of fashion and also a* **conversation piece**, *most of us found that it rather appallingly resembled a small, furry, dead creature.* (Page 81)

DATE #1: The first date with Hot Guy. *Vanessa couldn't wait until* **Date #1** *with Jeff the Hot Guy, even if he had suggested spearfishing as an activity.* (Pages 67–69, 87)

DR. D.: The unfortunate gentleman whose attempt to hit on my friends and me on Valentine's Day. His approach was used as an example of a bad pickup attempt in this book. His fatal flaw was making his sexual attraction to us ridiculously obvious, thereby lowering his value in our eyes. *Laughter didn't appear to be the reaction that* **Dr. D.** *was going for, judging by the speed with which he left our vicinity.* (Page 35)

DRINKING: The act of consuming alcoholic beverages. Should be kept to a minimum while picking up Hot Guys to alleviate any possibility of "beer goggles" altering your perceptions of said Hot Guys. *Emily knew she had been* **drinking** *too much when she realized her beer goggles were so strong she was attempting to pick up an octogenarian.* (Pages 57)

FOLLOW-UP: The term used to describe the conversation following the initial opener, or subsequent similar threads of conversation that can be used to continue the conversation if Hot Guy isn't forthcoming with responses. *Since Alan had responded with "Er" and "Um" to Cindy's opener, she decided to use her previously planned* **follow-up** *conversation starter, "What about chinchillas, do you think they are 'acceptable' rodents?"* (Pages 44–46, 49–51, 70, 75–76, 82)

GOOD ONE: A term used to describe the ideal guy, usually with the following characteristics (not necessarily in this order): Intelligent, Humorous, Honest, Ambitious, Friendly, Social, Fun, Good-Looking, Generous, Healthy, Sensitive. *Sally's mother, after meeting Grant, made a point of telling Sally on a daily basis that he was a **"good one"** and that she should marry him.* (Pages 87, 101)

HOT BARISTA GUY HANK: The very first guy I successfully approached. When I asked him what he was doing on Friday, he replied, "Hanging out with you." *Not even **Hot Barista Guy Hank***'s *ex-girlfriend's death threats could dampen my jubilation at having successfully picked up a guy.* (Pages 20–22, 23)

HOT GUY: Any guy who strikes your fancy, resulting in genuine curiosity about him, his life, what's in his pants, what kind of boyfriend/husband/domestic partner he'll make, et cetera, that leads to you want to meet him. The Hot Guy title does not refer universally to male models, rock stars, or professional athletes, but instead refers to whatever does it for you, the Hot Girl—whether that be killer abs, his obsession with B monster movies, or the way he treats his mother. *Tom could safely be considered a **Hot Guy**, despite his mullet.* (Page 12 and throughout the book)

HOTNESS SCALE: A scale against which a particular person's looks are rated. A rating of 10 is the very best, and 1 is the very worst. One person's 10 may be another person's 7—the scale is very subjective according to who is doing the rating. *Ethan was considered to be a 10 on the **hotness scale** by many of his female peers. Beth, however, put him somewhere around 5, because he was such a jackass.* (Pages 23–24)

LANDSCAPE: Refers to the general aesthetic rating of the people gathered at a particular place. *Dude, the* **landscape** *here is so much better than at that party down the street. Damn!* (Page 73)

MEAT MARKET: A term used to refer to a place, usually a bar or club, when the atmosphere is sexually charged. This is because everyone is checking everyone else out and sizing one another up to see if they would like to sleep with them; named for the resemblance to an emotionally devoid market selling slabs of meat. *Ugh, this place is a total* **meat market.** *I feel like at least twenty guys visually undressed us when we walked in.* (Here for reference only. Not mentioned in this book.)

NEED FOR INFORMATION: A type of opener, usually referring to a question one needs answered or an opinion to settle an argument. When delivered completely neutrally, this type of opener can never be construed by Hot Guy as a pickup attempt. Its very nature of being a piece of information one needs negates any possibility of it being mistaken as a sexual come-on. *Toby had left me a message ending with "See you around." There was a Hot Guy standing next to me, so I decided to pitch my question as a* **"need for information"** *opener.* (Pages 37–38, 40–42, 43)

NEUTRAL: A description that can only be applied to interactions where no sexual component exists. For example: *"Is that a mirror in your pocket? Because I can see myself in your pants,"* is not a **neutral** comment. *The sexual component exists so strongly in this situation that both parties are aware of the intentions of the person who delivered the message after only fifteen words.* (Page 36 and throughout the book)

OPENER (Also **OPENING**): The term used to describe the neutral conversation with a Hot Guy—usually only referring to the first two to three minutes of conversation. The opener can consist of a question of opinion to settle an argument or to answer a question you might have. It can be a need for information, a comment on a shared experience, or a combination of a shared experience and a need for information. The key component of the opener is that it should be neutral (i.e., containing no sexual component). Body language and delivery should be congruent. *Although Natalee's* **opener** *was flawlessly executed, she didn't walk away with a number. This was no fault of her own—it turned out Tyler liked guys, not girls.* (Page 37 and throughout the book)

PICKUP: The type of conversation initiation used with a guy you find attractive, with the intention of walking away with a date to meet the attractive guy at a later time. *That guy is so hot—watch me and my mad* **pickup** *skills go and get a date!* (Page 12 and throughout the book)

PORN: A multibillion-dollar industry based solely on the sexual inclinations of the (usually male) reproductive organ, whose owner wields a credit card. In this context, porn is used as an example to prove the point that whatever physical attributes you have, there is a porn site out there devoted to it. Guys wouldn't spend money on something that didn't turn them on, so it is 100 percent accurate to assume that if you've got it, there are guys out there who are into it. *Michelle had always thought her big feet to be a negatively viewed trait—until she found the* **porn** *site ILoveBigFeet.com.* (Pages 92–93)

PROXIMITY: The maneuvering of one's self to the proper location in order to open Hot Guy. The key rule of proximity is that there always needs to be another plausible and obvious reason to be so close to the target, such as ordering a drink, getting a napkin, checking your voice mail on your cell phone, going to the jukebox, and so forth. It should be done neutrally, so that Hot Guy does not suspect in the slightest that one is in his vicinity for the sole reason of speaking to him. *I was having difficulty gaining* **proximity** *to Hot Guy. This was because we were in a grocery store and he kept turning into new aisles just as I caught up to him. When I finally delivered my opener, he was fifteen feet away, and I found myself bellowing in order to be heard.* (Pages 43–44, 46–48, 49, 70, 82)

RAPPORT: Part of the post-opening conversation, this is the part where a connection is forged with Hot Guy so that one ceases to become "just another girl" and becomes someone Hot Guy wants to see again because he feels connected. When building a connection, one focuses the conversation more on Hot Guy with the purpose of finding out more about him, rather than just providing entertaining and likable details about one's self (as in the "This is a girl I want to get to know" phase). Rapport occurs directly after the two or three minutes of fun, entertaining filler. *Sandy found that Tom was rather tiring of her entertaining stories about being a lifeguard, so she decided to start building* **rapport**. (Pages 63, 64, 66–67, 80)

RYAN MASTERS: The guy who brutally rejected my proposal for him to accompany me to the Sadie Hawkins dance, which I had planned for the sole purpose of asking him. *I didn't even know where* **Ryan Masters** *lived, which is why I found his claim that I was a stalker completely unwarranted.* (Pages 15–20)

SHAKESPEARE: The teacup Chihuahua I borrowed from my friend for the purpose of picking up guys on the beach, as suggested by some asinine advice I had read. *For a creature with four-inch legs,* **Shakespeare** *could really cover some ground when he wanted to.* (Pages 28–30)

SHARED EXPERIENCE: Can be used to open Hot Guy when one references a common experience that you both just shared. The experience can be strange, humorous, abnormal, unexpected, or intellectual. This is not a recommended opening tactic, as guys have been using this trick to open girls for centuries (e.g., "Isn't it a beautiful night?") and may recognize it as a pickup. These are best used in conjunction with other types of openers, such as a need for information. *Although it worked out in the end, Stephanie knew that Greg had figured out she was hitting on him when he said, "That's just was I was going to say to you . . ." after she referenced their* **shared experience** *of being thrown overboard when the pleasure cruise capsized.* (Pages 37, 38–39, 42–43)

SIX-PACK (noun): Refers to the abdominal awesomeness on some Hot Guys, not a six-pack of beer. *Angie was distracted to the point of deafness upon viewing Eric's superb* **six-pack**. (Page 28)

"THIS IS A GIRL I WANT TO GET TO KNOW": The phrase that one hopes Hot Guy will think to himself as one entertains him with fun, interesting, entertaining stories. These stories can be things one saw in the news, things one saw in person, things that have happened, and so on. As part of the post-opening conversation, this part occurs directly after the opener and lasts for two or three minutes. *Cindy really hoped that Noah was still thinking,* **This is a girl I want to get to know**

after she had accidentally deposited the whole of her drink on his lap while demonstrating how she had looked while skydiving. (Pages 63–66)

WING (noun): A male or female friend who accompanies you in your approach to pick up a Hot Guy. You work with this person as a team to pick up the one you had your eye on. *Jeff, my male* **wing,** *failed to correctly introduce me into the group of guys he had opened for me because he was distracted by the game on the bar's TV.* (Pages 70–74)

Acknowledgments

THERE are so many people to thank!

To Matthew Lore, and everyone else at The Experiment—thank you for your wisdom, for your guidance, for loving this project so much, and for taking a chance on an unknown author. You made my pie-in-the-sky dreams come true! Thank you to everyone else who worked on the book: Jamie McNeely Quirk and Ann Kirschner for their editorial acumen, Pauline Neuwirth and Michael Fusco for their design work, and Rose Carrano for her publicity expertise.

To Vicki, for your insight and generous guidance, and most of all for being my lucky charm. Thank you times a million. To Bruce, for being such a massive part of the beginning of this journey and for letting me pick your brain on the art of male pickup.

To Vitamin R, Jenn F., RyLew, Erin S., Katie A., Mel M., Sarah T., Drew M., Kimberly I., Mary S., Jacques A., Becca S., Jess K., Lindsay J., Anne-Louise M., Leslie T., Angie M., Sage

W., Elise L., George S., Brad B., Leslie N. and Will S. for being so incredibly supportive and for the best and coolest friends anyone could ask for. Thanks for all the laughs, for all the support, and for all the listening. I wouldn't have made it this far without you.

A special thanks to Fitzy for being my acting coach and director, and for being my partner in crime on the way-out-of-my-comfort-zone path to YouTube. Also to Kimberly and Angie for sharing their acting expertise. You guys are awesome.

To Hugh Hamilton of Hugh Hamilton Photography and Ozzie at LuxeLab for making my author photograph a pleasurable experience. You guys did a great job. Thank you!

To Mom; Gramma Lynn; Dad; Megs; Gramma and Grandpa; the Garrett family; the Pollock family; Uncle Dennis; the Whitehead family; and KT, Brandon, and Eric for your love, never-ending excitement, and undying support.

To Grandpa Jack for thinking the title was cool, and for acting as my legal counsel.

To Brigitte, David, Elise, Sage, Riley, Leslie, and Eagle for being so excited with me and for throwing an impromptu party when I heard the news I was actually going to be published.

To Sage, Elise and Riley: Thank you for letting us live in your garage, for sharing your home, and for being **the coolest, nicest, most awesome family I've ever met. You guys rock.**

To Becca and Natalie for helping me come up with the best title ever.

To all my readers: Mom (especially Mom), Mary, Mel, Katie, Becca, Eagle, and Brigitte—I couldn't have done this without you.

To Lisa of KidSwim, Inc., for being so excited and for your wonderful friendship.

To the entire crew at Gooding & Company, for being the best office I've ever worked in and for all your advice, cheerleading, and support.

To the Heart & Pole girls: Thank you for showing me a side of myself I didn't realize was there. You guys are amazing.

To the crew at Michael Folonis, FAIA, & Associates—Michael, Rudy, Tracy, and Daniel—and to the crew (past and current) at Gladstein, Neandross & Associates: thanks for your excitement, encouragement, and support—and especially to Bob for being the first one to want a copy.

To the authors who have both inspired me and given me countless hours of blissful escapist therapy: Diana Gabaldon, Stephenie Meyer, Douglas Preston/Lincoln Child, James Rollins, Nora Roberts, Philippa Gregory, Laurell K. Hamilton, Michael Crichton, Stephen King, and Megan McCafferty.

To all the boys I had crushes on who never asked me out—you were my inspiration.

And most of all to Eagle—for all the encouragement, for all the hugs, for all the listening, for letting me tap your excellent editing skills, and for always, always being there. You're awesome, and I love you.

About the Author

When Samantha Scholfield isn't trying to improve the dating lives of the female population, she spends her free time people watching, taking pole-dancing classes, and hanging out with her boyfriend, whom she met using the techniques in this book. She lives in Seattle and has an English degree from UCLA. This is her first book.